FISH'S CLINICAL PSYCHOPATHOLOGY

Fish's Clinical Psychopathology

Signs and Symptoms in Psychiatry

Revised Reprint

Edited by
MAX HAMILTON
MD, FRCP, FRCPsych, FBPsS
Nuffield Professor of Psychiatry
University of Leeds

 BRISTOL: JOHN WRIGHT & SONS LTD. 1974

First printed 1967
Revised reprint 1974
Reprinted 1976
Reprinted 1978
Reprinted 1980
Reprinted, 1981

ISBN 0 7236 0371 5

Printed in Great Britain by John Wright and Sons Ltd.
at the Stonebridge Press, Bristol BS4 5NU

PREFACE TO THE FIRST EDITION

PROFESSOR GEORGE SISLER, Chairman of the Department of Psychiatry of the University of Manitoba, was kind enough to invite me to hold a series of seminars in his Department on the phenomenology of mental illness. This forced me to bring together the classic descriptions of psychiatric symptoms which are not easily found in the English literature. As the seminars were well received it seemed to me that a short book on psychiatric signs and symptoms would partly help fill a gap in the English literature.

This book has been written from the descriptive standpoint and therefore over-emphasizes certain aspects of psychiatry. This does not imply that the author believes that interpretative psychology, such as Freudian psychopathology, and experimental psychology have nothing to contribute to our understanding of psychiatric signs and symptoms. The aim of this book is to provide the postgraduate student with a detailed account of psychiatric symptomatology which will provide a firm basis for clinical work and research.

Thanks are due to Allyn and Bacon Inc. for permission to quote from *Principles of Psychology*, by J. Deese; to Penguin Books for permission to quote from *The Life of St. Teresa of Avila by Herself* (trans. J. M. Cohen); and to Tavistock Publications for permission to quote from *Personality and Personal Illness*, by G. A. Foulds.

FRANK FISH

EDITOR'S NOTE

FRANK FISH devoted his professional life to the principle that the fundamental basis of psychiatry lay in the careful, skilled and understanding observation of patients. He taught that observation had to be distinguished from theorizing and inference, for without that all the rest of psychiatry, from biochemistry and genetics to sociology and psycho-dynamics, floats in the air without a base.

His early death robbed British psychiatry of one of its greatest clinicians and German psychiatry of one of its great expositors. His memorial is to be found in the students who learned from him and in his writings, especially the three books which he wrote towards the end of his life. They are now out of print, and on me has fallen the privilege of revising and updating them. In doing so I have tried to retain their original style and outlook. I would like to think that such changes that I have introduced would have been acceptable to him.

MAX HAMILTON
Leeds, England
July 1974

CONTENTS

Chapter 1

Introduction

THE aim of this book is to describe in an objective way the signs and symptoms which occur in neuropsychiatric disorders. Anyone who is acquainted with Anglo-American psychiatric literature will know that the careful description of psychiatric signs and symptoms in English is conspicuous by its absence. The textbook *An Outline of Psychiatry*, by F. J. Fish, contains a detailed section on general symptomatology and this book can be regarded as an expansion of the account given there. It contains, however, additional material and is of course directed towards a different audience. With the growth of psychopharmacology and the development of biochemical and neurophysiological research, the need for careful description of clinical phenomena in psychiatry is greater than ever before. Without good clinical knowledge research in psychiatry will be fruitless.

The publication of a translation of Jaspers's *Allgemeine Psychopathologie* (*General Psychopathology*) gave British and American psychiatrists access for the first time to the classic German descriptions of psychiatric signs and symptoms. It is, however, unfortunate that this should be the only account of German views on symptomatology in English, because the book is overloaded with philosophy, is somewhat out of date, and does not do justice to the views which Jaspers does not accept. It is to be hoped that this present book will give the postgraduate student in psychiatry and clinical psychology a reasonable account of psychiatric symptoms and signs, but where necessary, theoretical concepts not well known in English are also briefly discussed.

This chapter will be concerned with general considerations and the next chapter will deal with the classification of psychiatric disorders. These two chapters are a necessary background to a discussion of psychiatric symptoms.

Before psychological phenomena can be discussed it is necessary to realize the philosophical problems involved. It is a fair assumption that the world around us exists independently of us, that it is material or composed of matter, and that it is not a product of our minds. Matter can be organized in a large number of ways and each new mode of organization has its own system of laws. When we consider the relationships which discrete units of matter make with each other we have the science of physics. When we investigate the way in which matter behaves when organized in the form of semi-permanent compounds we are in the realm of chemistry. However, matter can be organized into very complicated compounds which are autonomous and self-creative. The science which deals with matter of this kind is biology and that which deals with the interrelations of the parts of a living unit is physiology. Some living things develop a very complex variable relationship with the environment by means of a highly organized nervous system. The physical and chemical aspects of the nervous system are investigated by the neurophysiologist, while the psychologist investigates the behaviour of the animal as a whole. As we pass from the simpler forms of the organization of matter to the most complicated ones, new scientific disciplines appear at certain points. Each new science incorporates the laws of the science dealing with simpler forms of material organization, but also has new laws of its own which are not entirely explained by the preceding scientific discipline. Thus we can never reduce biology to physics and chemistry, or explain psychology entirely by means of neurophysiology.

Psychiatry is concerned with pathological human psychology, but frequent attempts have been made to reduce it to morbid neurophysiology. The neurophysiological findings in some diseases, e.g. general paresis, cannot be neglected by the psychiatrist, but it is not legitimate to attempt to explain all psychological problems by means of neurophysiology. Some human behaviour can only be explained as a complex interaction of the human being with his physical and social environment, involving laws and concepts which include, but go beyond, those of neurophysiology.

The problems of animal psychology are complex enough, but human psychology has to deal with the added complication of consciousness. The human being has some degree of awareness of his behaviour or, to put it another way, human behaviour is usually accompanied by some event in consciousness which the individual experiences as causing the behaviour. It can easily be shown that this conscious event and the behavioural act it accompanies do not always have a cause–effect relationship. This does not mean that we should reject all knowledge based on introspection, although we should treat it with caution.

By means of introspective knowledge of our own behaviour and practical experience of the behaviour of others, we develop a special body of psychological knowledge which can be called 'empathic psychology'. In order to make adequate contact with another person we must think ourselves into his situation and try to understand why he is behaving in a certain way. We all use empathic psychology, but those of us whose work consists in dealing with other people use it more frequently and our efficiency in our work may be directly related to our ability to understand our fellows. Nevertheless, our ability to empathize is limited to experiences which we have in common with others. Our empathy fails, therefore, with some of our patients who undergo experiences outside the normal range, e.g. certain ecstatic states.

The psychiatrist who is treating the psychologically ill cannot be satisfied with the simple empathic psychology of the intelligent sympathetic layman, since he is obliged to organize the knowledge he acquires in treating a patient in a way that can be used to help similar patients in the future. This leads to the creation of an interpretative psychology in which the ideas which have been obtained by empathizing with the patient are formulated in terms of some general theory which has been derived from neurophysiology, neurology, philosophy or mythology, usually the last two.

Interpretative and empathic psychology must be clearly distinguished from scientific psychology, which investigates animal and human behaviour in a scientific way and establishes rules and laws. In this it is quite different from the other two varieties of psychology in which the observer is inextricably entangled in the problem that he is investigating. In these types of psychology it is legitimate to assume that if two events are frequently found to follow in a given order then there is probably a causal connexion between them, but this is only an assumption and can only be proved by scientific investigation. Thus concepts developed by empathic and interpretative psychology can at times be put in a testable form and can be investigated by scientific psychology. There is therefore no impenetrable barrier between scientific psychology, on the one hand, and the empathic and interpretative psychologies, on the other. Concepts which have been developed by scientific psychology can be borrowed by interpretative psychology and may prove useful in psychotherapy. This two-way exchange between these two basically different varieties of psychology is very beneficial to both, but the psychiatrist must always take care that he is aware of the variety of psychology that he is using in any given case.

Many psychiatrists educated in the psychodynamic schools of psychiatry find difficulty in distinguishing between empathic psychology and interpretative psychology. In the first variety of psychology one simply tries to understand the patient by putting oneself in his position, while in the second variety one interprets what the patient says and does in terms of some set of concepts which have been found useful in the treatment of patients. These interpretations are not explanations in a scientific sense, but are working hypotheses which help the therapist to organize the information which he gets from the patient.

The lack of a philosophical training leads many English-speaking psychiatrists to confuse interpretations of content with explanations of form. In this book the main emphasis will be on the form of the psychiatric sign or symptom, not on the content. However, many psychodynamic psychiatrists believe that once they have interpreted the content of a symptom they have explained the form of the symptom. This is of course not so. For example, a woman may have the perverse desire to perform fellatio or she may be obsessed with the idea of the possibility of performing fellatio with God Almighty. In both cases the content concerns fellatio and a psychoanalyst could trace this back to an oral fixation. The form of the symptoms is, however, quite different as the first patient enjoys fellatio while the second is unable to free herself from an unpleasant thought. To interpret both symptoms as the result of oral fixation does not explain the difference in form.

Before proceeding to discuss classification we must consider the use of the term 'phenomenology'. As this is derived from certain philosophical concepts a short digression on philosophy is necessary. The basic philosophical problem is what is the relation between mind and matter. All philosophies are based on variations on the following three possible answers:

1. Mind is a product of matter functioning in a special way. This materialist solution of the problem leads to the conclusion that all psychological events are determined by matter.

2. Mind is primary and matter is a product of mind. This is the idealist position and leads to the conclusion that psychological events are primary or deducible from non-material events.

3. There is insufficient evidence to decide the answer to the problem. Since the only source of information is the sensations, it is possible to behave as if they were produced by matter. This is the empiricist position and is really a sort of practical materialism which dissociates itself from philosophical materialism, which naturally leads to religious disbelief.

Kant dealt with the problem of the relation of mind to matter by postulating that we experience the surface of the thing or phenomenon, but not the thing-in-itself or noumenon. This hidden thing-in-itself is usually called *Ding an sich* in philosophical discussions. In order to know the thing-in-itself the mind has to make a transcendental leap. Knowledge is therefore the result of sensations and the activity of the mind that organizes them in time and space, with the help of *a priori* categories of quantity, quality, relation, and modality. Kant called the scientific study of man, of which psychology was a part, 'Anthropology'. The term 'anthropology' is still used in German psychological and psychiatric literature to mean this general study of man and the unsophisticated English reader may be puzzled by the way certain German psychiatrists use the word, which in English means scientific, social or physical anthropology and not a philosophical speculation about man in general. From what has been said it will be obvious that Kant regarded psychology as a science which deals with the external aspects or phenomena of the mind, but not the mind itself.

Kant's idealist philosophy had a marked influence on philosophy and psychology, and echoes of his ideas can be found in nearly all German schools of psychology. At the beginning of the twentieth century Husserl introduced the idea that phenomenology, or the study of subjective psychological events, was the science that preceded all others. He considered that phenomenology described the form and content of subjective psychological experiences, and that psychology explained these experiences and their causal relationships. Dilthey introduced the concept of understanding into psychology and pointed out the need in psychology to understand the individual as a whole. He contrasted this with the analytical explanatory methods of natural science which he considered did not apply to psychology. He believed that psychology was a descriptive science and could never be an explanatory one.

The concepts of phenomenology and understanding were introduced into psychiatry by Karl Jaspers before he gave up that specialty for philosophy. His book *General Psychopathology* had a profound effect on German psychiatry but little or no effect in English-speaking countries. Jaspers considered that the task of phenomenology in psychiatry was to depict as clearly as possible the various psychological conditions as they are experienced by the patient. He did not believe that it was possible to describe those states exactly as the individual experienced them because the observer was not studying a physical object. However, Ludwig Binswanger has claimed that it is possible to experience the symptoms in the same way as the patient, but it is difficult to see how this is possible.

Binswanger elaborated an existentialist interpretative psychology by formulating morbid and abnormal psychological experiences in terms of the existentialist philosophy of Heidegger. This has not met with this philosopher's approval and Jaspers has called it 'a philosophical error'. Binswanger has called this existentialist reformulation of psychopathological experiences 'phenomenology'. Thus we see that this term is used in two quite different senses, so that for this reason alone it is best rejected. Quite apart from this, the term implies an acceptance of neo-Kantian or Heideggerian philosophy, neither of which is, in the opinion of the author, of much help to the clinical psychiatrists. It is for these reasons that the term 'phenomenology' will not be used in this book.

There are some other problems of terminology which must be considered. These are the use of the terms 'abnormal', 'morbid', 'psychogenic' and 'hysterical'. 'Normal' and 'abnormal' are used with different connotations and it is important to distinguish between them. Usually 'normal' is used to mean what is common and 'abnormal' what is uncommon or rare; this is the 'statistical' meaning. For example, an adult man of 2·2 metres in height is said to be abnormally tall. The other use is quite different. For example, in England there are relatively few persons who have a complete set of undamaged teeth. Nobody would use the term 'abnormal' to describe such persons and 'normal' to describe the average person with his incomplete set of carious teeth. Here the term 'normal' is used to signify an ideal. It is in this sense that the psycho-analysts state that we are all neurotic and therefore not 'normal'. In medicine, 'abnormal' has the additional connotation of signifying 'morbid' or 'diseased'. The abnormally tall person is likely to have an excess of circulating growth hormone and in many such individuals a tumour of the pituitary gland can be found to account for this excess. In psychiatry it is fair to say that all of the symptoms manifested by patients can be found occasionally or in some small degree in 'normal' people; much the same can be said for personality types or traits. It is the severity and frequency of these symptoms which makes them 'abnormal'. In some cases it can be demonstrated that the presence of these symptoms is related to coarse brain disease; in others, it is assumed that there is present some underlying but unknown neuro-physiological disorder.

Personality traits vary from one individual to another in the level or intensity of their manifestation. For many of them the majority of individuals have these traits in moderate degree and a lesser number show them in milder or more intense form. The frequency distribution of these traits therefore resembles the Gaussian or 'normal' distribution. For example, it may be that proneness to anxiety under stress is normally distributed in the bulk of the general population, but there is a small group in which slight stress produces severe anxiety. This would give us the usual bell-shaped curve up to a certain point, after which the incidence curve would rise once more. It would therefore resemble the distribution of intelligence in the general population, which follows the typical Gaussian curve until the lower levels of intelligence are reached, when a rise in the incidence of low intelligence occurs as a result of inherited or acquired brain damage. In this book it will be assumed that personality traits and the predisposition to abnormal psychiatric symptoms are normally distributed in the general population, if the effects of coarse brain disease are excluded. It may well be, however, that this assumption is not correct.

The term 'psychogenic' is often loosely used by internists and surgeons to mean 'no indication of physical disease has so far been discovered'. A psychogenic disorder is one in which a psychological trauma has given rise to a psychological abnormality. A good example of a psychogenic disorder is the wild chaotic behaviour which occurs in some patients after a very unpleasant experience which threatens the patient's life. This is not hysterical because there is no gain from the symptoms and in fact the abnormal behaviour may increase the risk to the patient's life. A hysterical symptom is adopted by the patient for the sake of some advantage, although he is not fully aware of this motivation. The essential feature of the hysterical symptom is that it is goal-directed, i.e. the patient is obtaining some advantage from it although he is not conscious that this is so. Some English-speaking psychiatrists use the term 'psychogenic' as a synonym for 'hysterical', but this is obviously incorrect. While hysterical symptoms are necessarily psychogenic, not all psychogenic symptoms are hysterical.

Chapter 2

The Classification of Psychiatric Disorders

ANY discussion of the classification of psychiatric disorders must begin with the frank admission that the final classification of disease must be based on aetiology. Until we know the causation of mental illnesses, we must use some variety of classification which helps us to care for our patients and which does not obstruct research. In physical medicine syndromes existed long before the aetiology of these illnesses was known. Some of these syndromes have subsequently been shown to be true disease entities because they are always produced by one essential cause. Thus small-pox and measles were carefully described and differentiated by the Arabian physician Rhazes in the tenth century A.D. With each new step in the progress of medicine, such as auscultation, percussion, microscopy, bacteriology, radiology, immunology, biochemistry and electrophysiology, some syndromes have been found to be true disease entities, while others have been split into such entities. For example, diabetes mellitus has been shown to be a syndrome which can have several different aetiologies. It therefore seems logical that what we must do in psychiatry is to establish syndromes in order to organize our knowledge, but we must not forget that they may or may not be true disease entities.

Now let us consider the nature of syndromes in general, and the different syndromes which exist in psychiatry. A syndrome is a constellation of symptoms which is unique as a group. It may, of course, contain symptoms which occur in other syndromes, but it is the particular combination of symptoms which makes the syndrome specific. In psychiatry, as in general medicine, many syndromes began as one striking sign or symptom. Thus in the nineteenth century stupor, furore and hallucinosis were syndromes based on one striking symptom. Later the frequent simultaneous occurrence of signs and symptoms led to the establishment of true syndromes. For example, Korsakoff described the amnestic syndrome as a disorder of impressibility and confabulation. Later this syndrome was found to consist of disorientation for time and place, euphoria, difficulty in registration, confabulation and 'tram-line' thinking. Later it was discovered that in the alcoholic amnestic state there is always severe damage to the mammillary bodies, so that today the alcoholic Korsakoff state is a true disease entity with a neuro-pathological basis.

7

Sometimes in psychiatry the symptoms of the syndrome seem to have a meaningful coherence. For example, in mania the cheerfulness, the overactivity, the pressure of talk, and the flight of ideas can all be understood as arising from the elevated mood. In other cases the signs and symptoms have one common aspect. Thus the gross motor disorders in the absence of coarse brain disease distinguish the catatonic syndrome from other functional mental disorders. The fact that we can understand or empathize with our patients has led to the distinction between primary symptoms which are alleged to be the immediate result of the disease process and secondary ones which are a psychological elaboration of or reaction to primary symptoms. The term 'primary symptom' or 'primary sign' is also used for symptoms which cannot be derived from any other psychological event.

The first major classification of mental illness was based on the distinction between disorders arising from disease of the brain and those with no such basis, i.e., organic versus functional states. These words are still used, but like so many in psychiatry they have lost their original meaning. For example, epilepsy and its associated behavioural disorders, is always regarded as 'organic', yet in the majority of cases the only link with the brain is passages that are found in the E.E.G., which indicate changes in activity, i.e. function. Sometimes, of course, brain disease produces a clear clinical picture of a 'functional' mental illness, which gives us the logical absurdity of a functional illness (i.e. non-organic) of organic origin. Schizophrenia and manic-depression are the great examples of 'functional' disorders, but the evidence of genetics shows that there must be some organic basis to them. In their literal meaning, these categories of classification are absurd, but they retain their usefulness because the syndromes so classified can be distinguished and the distinction is one of the clearest in psychiatry.

The syndromes due to brain disorders can be classified into acute, subacute and chronic. In acute organic syndromes the commonest feature is alteration of consciousness, which can be dream-like, depressed or restricted. This gives four acute organic syndromes, viz. delirium, the subacute delirious state, organic stupor or torpor, and the twilight state.

All these syndromes have in common disorientation, incoherence of psychic life, and some degree of anterograde amnesia. In delirium there is a dream-like change in consciousness so that the patient is unable to distinguish between mental images and perceptions. This leads to hallucinations and illusions. Usually there is also severe anxiety and restlessness. In the subacute delirious state there is a general lowering of awareness and a marked incoherence of psychological activity, so that the patient is bewildered and perplexed. Hallucinations, illusions, and delusions occur, but they are more or less isolated. The level of awareness varies considerably and tends to be lowered at night. In organic stupor or torpor the level of consciousness is generally lowered and the patient responds poorly or not at all to stimuli. After recovery the patient usually has little or no idea of the events which occurred during his illness. The subacute delirious state can be regarded as a transitional form between delirium proper and organic stupor. In the organic twilight state consciousness is restricted so that the mind is dominated by a small group of ideas, attitudes, and images. These patients may appear to be perplexed, but often their behaviour is well ordered and they can carry out complicated patterns of behaviour.

There are two acute organic syndromes in which consciousness is not obviously disordered, viz., organic hallucinosis and the acute organic paranoid state. In organic hallucinosis the patient hears abusive, threatening hallucinatory voices in a state of clear consciousness. Delusions of persecution, which are the direct result of the hallucinatory voices, are also present. In the acute organic paranoid state delusions of persecution occur in the setting of clear consciousness in the presence of some acute physical illness such as cardiac infarction. This syndrome is probably the result of disinhibition by the physical illness of a normally hidden suspicious attitude.

The characteristic subacute organic state is, of course, the amnestic or Korsakoff syndrome, the symptoms of which we have already outlined as an example of a syndrome (see p. 8). The other subacute syndrome is 'organic neurasthenia', which is a neurotic-like illness in which there is undue fatigue, depression, anxiety, irritability, headache, dizziness and intolerance of noise. This may occur during the recovery from organic states, when it is transient, or in association with chronic physical diseases such as pulmonary tuberculosis, or in permanent non-progressive brain damage, for example after closed head injury or encephalitis.

The typical chronic organic syndrome is dementia, in which there is a deterioration of the personality, loss of memory, and loss of intelligence. If the underlying morbid process cannot be arrested utter mindlessness and death are the final outcome.

There are several well-known focal syndromes, but the frontal lobe syndrome is probably the best known. These patients have a general lack of drive, lack of foresight, inability to plan ahead, and an indifference to the feelings of others. There is also a happy-go-lucky carelessness and a silly facetious type of humour, the so-called Witzelsucht.

Before we consider the functional mental disorders we should consider the use of the word 'functional'. It would be more correct to describe the functional psychological disorders as those in which we have been unable to discover any coarse brain disease, but in some of which it is highly likely that we will find some finer variety of brain disease. Nevertheless, all the evidence indicates that, in some disorders, such changes in the brain could play only a small part in the total picture. The only adjective which seems suitable to convey this meaning is the word 'functional'. In the remainder of this discussion the word will be used in this limited sense of mental disorders not caused by coarse brain disease.

It is customary to divide the functional mental diseases into neuroses and psychoses. The neurotic has insight into his illness, has only a part of his personality involved in the disorder, can distinguish between his subjective experiences and reality, and does not construct a false environment based on his misconceptions. The psychotic, on the other hand, lacks insight, has the whole of his personality distorted by illness, and constructs a false environment out of his subjective experiences. Other distinguishing points are that the psychotic has a gross disorder of basic drives, including that of self-preservation, and unlike the neurotic is unable to make a reasonable social adjustment. There is in fact no criterion which will allow to make a clear distinction between psychosis and neurosis. Hysteria is, of course, a typical neurosis, but one can find hysterics with grossly abnormal personalities, with no insight, unable to work, living in a world of fantasy, and making suicidal attempts. On the other hand, one can find severe depressive illnesses in which the patient knows he is ill and asks for treatment, and schizophrenic illnesses which do not prevent the patient from earning his living.

Many psychiatrists use the terms 'psychotic' and 'neurotic' to mean no more than severe and mild, an inexcusable use of jargon instead of plain English. It would be better if these terms were abandoned since they produce nothing but confusion. Discussions on them have a peculiar medieval flavour, heightened by a plethora of pontifical ex-cathedra statements.

Jaspers regards the neurotic as someone who has an abnormal response to his difficulties in which some specific mechanism has transformed his experiences. For example, in hysteria the mechanism of dissociation is used in this way. Since we can all use this particular mechanism, the difference between the hysteric and the normal is one of degree. As Schneider has suggested, we can regard the neuroses and personality disorders as variations of human existence which differ from the norm quantitatively rather than qualitatively. While this seems to be a reasonable way of regarding most personality disorders and neuroses, it does not seem that obsessional states can be regarded as a variation in human existence.

In the English-speaking world it is customary to separate off the neuroses from the personality abnormalities. In German-speaking countries, on the other hand, the neuroses are regarded as reactions of abnormal personalities to moderate or mild stress and the reaction of normal personalities to severe stress. In the term 'abnormal personality' the word 'abnormal' is not being used in the sense of 'morbid', but merely in the sense that the individual has one or more personality traits which lie outside the range which is generally regarded as normal in the particular society in which the patient lives. Since the word 'reaction' is used in many different ways it is necessary to discuss the way in which the term 'psychogenic reaction' is being used in this book. This term designates a reversible prolonged psychological response to psychological trauma which can be understood as the result of the effect of the causative event on the patient's personality. Thus acute anxiety states and hysteria can be regarded as varieties of psychogenic reaction provoked by stress and determined by the personality and cultural factors. Sometimes acute and more often chronic psychological trauma can produce an irreversible, abnormal psychological state when it acts upon a vulnerable personality. Such a condition may be a chronic anxiety state or it may be a personality development in which delusion-like ideas (*q.v.*) finally occur. In the personality development the abnormal personality traits create constant social and personal difficulties for the subject, giving rise to overvalued ideas (*q.v.*) which ultimately become delusional in intensity. A good example of the paranoid personality development is the syndrome of morbid jealousy. An insecure suspicious man with an unstable childhood background may develop ideas of jealousy about his wife, and as the stress of the marital situation continues, the ideas develop into delusions of marital infidelity. This concept of delusional states which are not due to the functional psychoses is not often used by English-speaking psychiatrists, but it can be useful in clinical work.

If one accepts Schneider's approach, then the neuroses, psychogenic reactions, personality developments, and abnormal personalities are not illnesses in the sense that there is a morbid process in the nervous system, while the functional psychoses are illnesses in this sense. This leads us out of the difficulty of defining the term 'psychosis' on the basis of symptomatology. The functional psychosis which leads to so much difficulty is so-called 'endogenous depression', in which there may be a morbid change in mood in the absence of delusions and in the presence of some insight. If we define 'psychosis' as a mental disorder in which there is a morbid process in the brain, then this problem is solved, but it creates two new ones. The main objection is that most English-speaking psychiatrists are accustomed to using the term 'psychosis' for severe mental illnesses in which delusions, hallucinations, or severe personality deteriorations are present, so that they will therefore have difficulty in calling a mild endogenous depression 'psychotic'. The other objection is that we are assuming that a morbid process exists in the functional psychoses and this has never been proved. The only reply to this is that many psychiatrists find it difficult to regard the functional psychoses which respond well to drugs and other physical methods of treatment as disorders which can be explained entirely on psychological grounds. This is a typical example of the confusion produced by the use of the terms 'psychosis' and 'neurosis'.

Now let us consider the classification of the functional psychoses. Schizophrenia was first isolated by Kraepelin, under the name of 'dementia praecox', as an illness which led to deterioration of the personality. Later

Bleuler introduced the term 'schizophrenia' and included in this illness many cases in which severe deterioration of the personality did not occur. This has led to the situation that in the New World and Switzerland any unusual functional psychiatric disorder is likely to be diagnosed as schizophrenia. Kraepelin also described manic-depressive insanity as an illness in which recovery occurred, although recurrence was common. Thus, by using the course of the illness as the main differentiating point, two major groups of functional psychoses were isolated, one in which the primary disorders appeared to be those of intellect, emotional expression, and volition, and the other in which the symptoms could all be explained on the basis of the abnormal mood.

It was soon realized that there were psychoses which were not primarily mood disorders but which were phasic, like manic-depressive insanity. Some psychiatrists considered them to be manic-depressive, while others included them in Bleuler's wide group of schizophrenias. A few psychiatrists took the view that as schizophrenia was an incurable illness and these schizophrenia-like functional psychoses recovered, they should be considered to be a separate group of illnesses. These psychoses were originally called 'degeneration psychoses' because it was believed that they occur mainly in degenerates or what today would be called 'psychopathic personalities'. Recently Leonhard, who has spent 30 years studying this group of disorders, has suggested the term 'cycloid psychosis' to indicate the phasic nature and the fact that they differ from the cyclic or manic depressive illnesses.

Since the cycloid psychoses will be referred to later in this book and Leonhard's views are not well known in English, a brief account of these psychoses will now be given. They are divided into three bipolar illnesses, viz. anxiety-happiness, confusion, and motility psychoses. Each illness has an excited and an inhibited pole. In any one phase of the psychosis the illness may be unipolar or may swing between the two poles. This distinguishes these psychoses from the non-systematic schizophrenias in which signs of excitement and inhibition occur side by side.

In the anxiety psychosis the patient is intensely anxious and usually has ideas of reference, hallucinatory voices, hypochondriacal delusions, and somatic hallucinations. In happiness psychosis the patient is ecstatic, believing that he is extremely fortunate and has a mission to help others.

The characteristic feature of confusion psychosis is confusion of thinking which is the result of an incoherence in the choice of theme. This leads the patient to introduce irrelevant material into his replies to questions. In the excited phase there is no connexion between successive sentences and replies to questions are completely irrelevant. In the inhibited phase the patient is perplexed and has poverty of speech. If the illness is very severe then there is a perplexed stupor. These perplexed patients with poverty of speech have often ideas of reference and apophanous ideas (*q.v.*). Leonhard insists that these symptoms are not diagnostic of schizophrenia when they occur in this setting of poverty of speech and perplexity.

The motility psychosis may be hyperkinetic or akinetic. The excited or hyperkinetic phase is more common than the akinetic and is characterized by excessive reactive and expressive movements which give rise to a clown-like or theatrical overactivity. Distortion and lack of grace of body movements, which are characteristics of catatonic excitement, are not seen. In the akinetic phase there is a pure akinesia and there are no signs of obstruction, catalepsy, stereotypies, impulsive excitements, or negativisim.

Kraepelin included in the group of manic-depressive insanity all those functional psychoses in which the mood disorder was primary. He also recognized that sometimes the phase of the illness could be very mild and be misdiagnosed as a neurosis. In many cases of manic-depressive illness, mania and depression alternated during one phase of the illness or occurred at different times of life. In such patients a family history of mild mood disorders and manic-depressive illnesses was common. However, cases of severe depression occur in which there is no family history of manic-depressive insanity and no manic symptoms ever occur during the depression or at any other time of life. These illnesses have been called 'endogenous depression' and not all psychiatrists believe that they should be classified as manic-depressive. It seems probable that there is a large heterogeneous group of affective psychoses out of which we can separate such disorders as manic-depressive illnesses, endogenous depressions, involutional depressions, and so on.

For the sake of completeness we should consider the classification of mental subnormality. This falls into two main groups, viz. subcultural mental subnormality and childhood organic states. Subcultural mental subnormality includes those individuals who are at the lower end of the normal distribution curve for intelligence. In quite a number of these the abnormality of the personality is just as important as the deficiency of intelligence, so that it may be difficult to decide whether the patient should be classified as having an abnormal intellectual endowment or an abnormal personality. In either case, however, he will be classified under the heading of abnormal variation of mental life.

From what has been said we can now proceed to outline our classification, which is as follows.

1. Abnormal variations in mental life

a. Abnormal intellectual endowment
The subcultural mentally subnormal.

b. Abnormal personalities
    i. *Antisocial:* Psychopathic personalities in the Anglo-American sense.
    ii. *Abnormal personalities:* Not antisocial.

iii. *Abnormal personality developments:* These can be looked upon as a chronic response of an abnormal person to his life difficulties. The symptoms may be 'neurotic', taking the form of anxiety and hypochondriacal fears, or they may be 'psychotic'-like in the form of overvalued or delusion-like ideas of bodily ill health or marital infidelity.

c. Abnormal reactions to experience

The individual is reacting to some traumatic experience. He may be relatively normal, when the response will be one of fright or anxiety, or he may be abnormal, in which case a 'neurotic illness', such as hysteria, which is a goal-directed reaction, or a 'psychotic'-like illness, such as a paranoid reaction, may occur.

2. Mental illnesses

a. The functional psychoses

These are true illnesses in which a sharp break in the personality occurs, probably the result of a neurophysiological disorder which so far has escaped detection. If we divide them on the course of illness and the nature of the symptoms, we have three sub-groups:

    i. *The affective disorders.*
    ii. *The cycloid disorders.*
    iii. *The schizophrenias.*

b. The organic states

These are true illnesses. The psychiatric clinical picture is not usually specific to the morbid process. These illnesses can be further classified as physical diseases.

Chapter 3

Disorders of Perception

THESE can be divided into sensory distortions and sensory deceptions. In distortions there is a constant real perceptual object which is perceived in a distorted way, while in sensory deceptions a new perception occurs which may or may not be in response to an external stimulus.

I. SENSORY DISTORTIONS

There is a change in the perception which is the result of a change in the intensity and quality of the stimuli or the spatial form of the perception.

1. Changes in intensity (hyperaesthesia and hypoaesthesia)

Increased intensity of sensations, or hyperaesthesias, may be the result of intense emotions or a lowering of the physiological threshold. Thus a patient may see roof tiles as a brilliant flaming red or hear the noise of a door closing like the sound of a clap of thunder.

Some hypochondriacal personalities and neurotics are very sensitive to noise. This may be partly due to anxiety which is likely to increase the distracting effect of noise. However, some anxious and depressed patients complain that the voices of other people seem to come from a long way off. This is probably the effect of an anxious preoccupation with some problem making it difficult for the patient to concentrate on what is going on around him.

A true hypoacusis occurs in delirium where the threshold for all sensations is raised. The delirious patient also has a defect of attention which accentuates his perceptual difficulties. It is important to remember these facts when dealing with the delirious patient, because if one speaks slowly and loudly to such patients they are usually able to accept reassurance and to co-operate during physical examination and treatment procedures.

2. Changes in quality

These are mainly visual distortions brought about by toxic substances which colour all perceptions. Colourings of yellow, green and red have been named 'xanthopsia', 'chloropsia' and 'erythropsia'. The drug santonin used in the treatment of helminthiasis can produce violet or yellow vision. One patient taking santonin complained that his soup stank and that water tasted of lead. These were not hallucinations but qualitative changes of perception brought about by the drug.

15

3. Changes in spatial form (dysmegalopsia)

This naturally occurs in the visual field, when it is known as dysmegalopsia. Micropsia is a visual disorder in which the patient sees objects smaller or farther away than they really are. The opposite kind of visual distortion is known as macropsia, or megalopsia. This definition of micropsia includes the experience of the retreat of objects into the distance, without any change in size. This has, however, been called porropsia by some authors. The terms 'macropsia' and 'micropsia' have been used for the changes in the perception of size in dreams and hallucinations.

Dysmegalopsia can result from retinal disease, disorders of accommodations and convergence, and from temporal lobe lesions. In oedema of the retina the visual elements are separated so that the image falls on what is functionally a smaller part of the retina than usual. This gives rise to micropsia. Scarring of the retina with retraction naturally produces macropsia, but as the distortion produced by scarring is usually irregular metamorphopsia is more likely to result.

Complete paralysis of accommodation or overactivity of accommodation during near vision is likely to cause macropsia, while partial paralysis of accommodation will lead to the experience during near vision that the object is very near, i.e. micropsia will occur. Accommodation and convergence can be dissociated with a haptoscope. If accommodation is normal but convergence is weakened, macropsia occurs and vice versa. Kinnier Wilson described a simple experiment which shows the effect of accommodation. The subject looks at a book which is lying open on the table, shuts one eye, and interposes a finger between his eye and the book. He then fixes on the finger, whereupon the letters in the book become smaller.

Despite the fact that disorders of accommodation and convergence can cause dysmegalopsia, it is not common to meet cases in which the visual disorder is the result of a failure of these peripheral mechanisms. Occasionally dysmegalopsia occurs in poisoning with atropine or hyoscine. Although hypoxia and rapid acceleration of the body can disturb accommodation and convergence, dysmegalopsia is rare among high-altitude pilots. In 800 experiments in a decompression chamber only 1 case of dysmegalopsia occurred. Sometimes the nerves controlling accommodation are affected by disease. Thus a patient with chronic arachnoiditis affecting the optic chiasma had micropsia.

In fact dysmegalopsia is more common in central lesions, mainly those affecting the posterior part of the temporal lobe. Usually these distortions occur in attacks and may usher in a fit. Macropsia, micropsia, and gross irregular distortions may occur in all varieties of temporal lobe lesions.

II. SENSORY DECEPTIONS

These can be easily divided into illusions, which are misinterpretations of stimuli arising from an external object, and hallucinations, which are perceptions without an adequate external stimulus.

1. Illusions

In the illusions stimuli from a perceived object are combined with a mental image to produce a false perception. It is unfortunate that the word 'illusion' is also used for perceptions which do not agree with the physical stimuli, such as the Müller-Lyer illusion. It is customary to explain illusions as the result of set, lack of perceptual clarity, and intense emotions. In fact the intense emotions produce a set and may decrease perceptual acuity, so that we can derive illusions from set and lack of perceptual clarity. Illusions are not in themselves morbid as they can occur in normals, when they can, of course, usually be corrected. Thus the normal person walking along a dark lonely lane is mildly frightened and cannot see clearly. He is therefore likely to misinterpret innocuous shadows as threatening people. In delirium the perceptual threshold is raised and the patient is usually anxious and bewildered, so that illusions are quite common and the patient may perceive innocent gestures and actions of the doctor and the nurses as threats. Illusions occur in the severe depressive with delusions of guilt. He believes that he is wicked and deserving of punishment or death. He may therefore say that he hears people talking about killing him, that he hears the rattle of chains, and can see the flickering of the fire being prepared for burning him at the stake. The patient with delusions of self-reference misinterprets everything which he sees or hears. Thus he sees people making signs about him and he hears them talking about him. It is at times difficult to be certain whether the patient merely has the illusion that people are talking about him or whether he is actually hearing hallucinatory voices talking about him and attributing them to real people in his environment.

The classic psychiatrists described fantastic illusions in which the patient saw extraordinary modifications of his environment. Thus Griesinger had a patient who looked in the mirror and instead of seeing his own head he saw that of a pig. Professor Fish had a patient who insisted that during an interview he saw the psychiatrist's head change into that of a rabbit. This patient was given to exaggeration and confabulation. He also would invent non-existent puppies and tell other patients not to tread on the puppy. Fantastic illusions belong more in the works of James Thurber than in the realm of psychiatry.

One interesting type of illusion is pareidolia, in which vivid illusions occur without the patient making any effort. These illusions are the result of excessive fantasy thinking and a vivid impressive visual imagery. They cannot therefore be explained as the result of affect or set, so that they differ from the ordinary illusion. Pareidolias occur when the subject sees vivid pictures in the fire or in the clouds, without any conscious effort on his part and sometimes even against his will.

Illusions have to be distinguished from intellectual misinterpretation and from functional hallucinations. Thus when someone says that a piece of rock is a precious stone or that the doctor is not really a doctor

but the public prosecutor, this is an intellectual misinterpretation
Although the older German psychiatrists explained the misidentification
of persons as an intellectual disorder, the situation is not as clear as it
might seem at first sight. It is possible that misinterpretation in acute
schizophrenic shifts may be the result of an apophanous or delusional
perception (*see* p. 40) based on some alteration of perception.

The functional hallucination must be distinguished from an illusion. It
occurs as a response to an environmental stimulus, but both the provoking
stimulus and the hallucination are perceived by the patient, while the
stimuli from the environment in the illusion form an essential part of the
new perception.

2. Hallucinations

a. Definitions

Esquirol's original definition of the hallucination as 'a perception
without an object' has the advantage of being brief and to the point, but
it does not quite cover the functional hallucination. To cover this point
and to exclude dreams Jaspers suggested the following definition: 'A false
perception, which is not a sensory distortion or misinterpretation, but
which occurs at the same time as real perceptions.'

What distinguishes hallucinations from perceptions is that they come
from 'within', although the subject reacts to them as if they were true
perceptions coming from 'without'. This distinguishes them from vivid
mental images which also come from within but are recognized as such.
As with all abnormal mental phenomena, it is not possible to make an
absolute distinction. The individual with eidetic imagery will examine his
images as if they were truly external objects, and some patients have
sufficient insight to recognize that their hallucinations are not truly
objective.

Hillers has suggested that hallucinations in schizophrenia are neither
mental images nor true perceptions. He points out that schizophrenics
with hallucinations of smell and taste are not really perceiving smells or
tastes. For example, a patient said that his food tasted of arsenic, which is
tasteless and which he had never tasted. These facts were pointed out to
him, but he insisted that his food tasted of arsenic. Hillers argues that the
essential feature of a schizophrenic experience is 'the making of a
relationship without adequate proof' which is roughly the same as
Gruhle's definition of a schizophrenic delusion. He suggests that the
schizophrenic experience is not perceptual, but the patient is compelled
to formulate some of his experiences in a perceptual form.

A great deal of discussion has raged in the past about the concept of the
'pseudo-hallucination'. Most of the statements on pseudo-hallucinations
are derived from Jaspers, who obtained much of his information on the
subject from the writings of Kandinsky, who had experienced them
himself. Jaspers first of all distinguished between true perceptions and

mental images. The former are substantial (*leibhaftig*), appear in objective space, are clearly delineated, constant and independent of the will, and their sensory elements are full and fresh. Mental images are incomplete, not clearly delineated, dependent on the will, inconstant and have to be re-created. Pseudo-hallucinations are a type of mental image which although clear and vivid lack the substantiality (*Leibhaftigkeit*) of perceptions: they are seen in full consciousness, known to be not real perceptions and are not located in objective space but in subjective space. In his book *General Psychopathology* Jaspers gives only two examples. The first is obtained from Kandinsky who described the experience of a patient after taking a dose of tincture of opium. It would therefore seem unlikely that the pseudo-hallucinations appeared in full consciousness. The second is an account given by a patient, a 'chronic paranoic' who himself distinguished between hallucinatory voices and voices which he heard inwardly.

Sedman has studied pseudo-hallucinations very carefully and in one paper (Sedman, 1966) he has given a detailed review of the literature as well as an account of his investigation of 72 patients. He considers that he has confirmed the existence of pseudo-hallucinations as defined by Jaspers, but in his account of specific instances he describes several individuals who had experienced visual hallucinations which had all the characteristics of real perceptions, e.g. they appeared in objective space, but which they discovered afterwards were hallucinations. In some cases the patients knew at the time that they were not genuine perceptions. It is difficult to understand why these should have been called 'pseudo-hallucinations' as opposed to 'real visual hallucinations'.

Jaspers insisted that there is no gradual transition between the true and the pseudo-hallucination but, in fact, such transitions do occur. For example, one meets subjects who have non-substantial hallucinations which they experience as occurring in outer objective space and patients with substantial hallucinations which occur in outer space, but which they recognize as the result of their active, vivid imagination. There is also experimental work to show that subjects cannot differentiate between a faint image projected on to a screen and a mental image which they themselves have projected on to the same screen. The gulf which Jaspers claims to have found between perception and mental imagery is the result of his preconceived ideas and not derived from facts. This is confirmed by the work of Leff (1968) who studied the perceptual phenomena in subjects undergoing sensory deprivation. He found that the subjects could not always distinguish between images and hallucinations and concluded that the perceptual experiences of normal people under conditions of sensory deprivation overlapped considerably with those of mental patients. Hare (1973), in a brief review of the subject, considered that much of the alleged difference between real and pseudo-hallucinations depended on the absence or presence of insight. This is confirmed by the cases described by Sedman. He concluded that since insight was often fluctuating and partial, it was more profitable to think in terms of the degree of insight, in which case the concept of pseudo-hallucinations became largely superfluous. It may be also added that pseudo-hallucinations are alleged to be experienced sometimes by hysterical and attention-seeking personalities. In this respect it should be remembered, in the words of F. M. R. Walshe: 'It is not information that these patients wish to convey, but an impression that they wish to create'.

b. Causes

Hallucinations can be the result of intense emotions, suggestion, disorders of sense organs, sensory deprivation, and disorders of the central nervous system.

i. *Emotion:* Very depressed patients with delusions of guilt may hear voices reproaching them. These are not the continuous voices of paranoid schizophrenia or organic hallucinosis, but tend to be disjointed, saying separate words or short phrases such as 'rotter', 'kill yourself', and so on. These voices can be regarded as the voice of conscience. The occurrence of continuous persistent hallucinatory voices in severe depression should arouse the suspicion of schizophrenia or some intercurrent physical disease.

ii. *Suggestion:* Several experimenters have shown that normal subjects can be persuaded to hallucinate. Thus Seashore asked subjects to walk down a dimly lit corridor and stop when they saw a faint light appear over the door at the end. During several trials no light was switched on at the end of the corridor. Nevertheless most subjects stopped walking at some point and said that they could see a light.

Barber has shown that normal female subjects can be persuaded to hallucinate visually and auditorily either by hypnosis or by brief task-motivating instructions. This latter technique consists in asking the subject to try to hallucinate a tune or an animal and then telling her that she could do much better because most people can hallucinate if they try hard enough, so all she has to do is to try hard and control her mind. As a result of his own work and a comprehensive review of the literature Barber came to the conclusion that hypnotic hallucinations do not produce objective effects similar to those produced by ordinary perceptions, such as complementary after-images and so on. He concluded that: 'It appears parsimonious at the present time to categorize the suggested hallucination under the general psychological rubric of imagination rather than perception.'

Hysterics with severe behaviour disorders, as in the so-called 'hysterical psychosis', have visual hallucinations which fit in with their fantasy and cultural background. These patients see black men, frightening faces, and so on, or say they do.

It has been suggested that some patients with delusions of reference hallucinate as the result of their persecutory set. It would appear that they are either misinterpreting their environment and suffering from auditory illusions or they have a true hallucinosis, which is another sign of the illness causing the self-reference.

iii. *Disorder of a peripheral sense organ:* Hallucinatory voices may occur in ear disease and visual hallucinations in eye disease, but usually there is some disorder of the central nervous system as well. For example, a woman of 66 years of age suffered from glaucoma for 3 years and then began to have continuous visual hallucinations. At this time she showed evidence of arteriosclerotic dementia and had a focus of abnormal activity in the left posterior temporal lobe.

Peripheral lesions of sense organs may play a part in hallucinations in organic states. Thus it has been shown that negative scotomota are to be found in patients suffering from delirium tremens.

iv. *Sensory deprivation:* If all incoming stimuli are reduced to a minimum in a normal subject he will begin to hallucinate after a few hours. These are usually changing visual hallucinations and repetitive words and phrases. It has been suggested that the sensory isolation produced by deafness may cause paranoid disorders in the deaf, but investigations have so far not been conclusive.

An interesting psychosis produced in human beings by sensory deprivation is 'black-patch disease' or delirium following cataract extraction in the aged. After the operation both eyes are bandaged for several days and the patient often begins to hallucinate. This is probably the result of sensory deprivation and mild senile brain changes. There is an interesting case on record of a patient who had 'black-patch disease' after one operation and was frightened by the prospect of an operation on her other eye a few years later. She was reassured by a psychiatrist who saw her before the operation and immediately afterwards, and promised to see her whenever she asked for him during the postoperative period. After the second operation she had no hallucinations of any kind.

v. *Disorders of the central nervous system:* Lesions of the diencephalon and the cortex can produce hallucinations which are usually visual, but can be auditory.

Hypnagogic and hypnopompic hallucinations can be regarded as special varieties of organic hallucinations. Hypnagogic hallucinations occur when the subject is falling asleep and hypnopompic when the subject is waking up. It is likely that hypnopompic hallucinations are really hypnagogic which occur in the morning when the subject is waking and drowsing off, so that they actually happen when he is falling asleep. It has been suggested that the term 'hypnopompic' should be retained for hallucinations persisting from sleep when the eyes are open.

Hypnagogic hallucinations occur during drowsiness, are discontinuous, appear to force themselves on the subject, and do not form part of an experience in which the subject participates as he does in a dream. McKellar and Simpson found hypnagogic hallucinations in 115 of a group of 182 students (63·18 per cent). The commonest hallucinations in their series were auditory, which occurred in 78 subjects. These were followed by visual hallucinations, which were found in 64 subjects. This contradicts most other findings in which visual hypnagogic hallucinations were the commonest kind. McKellar and Simpson found kinaesthetic hallucinations in 13 of their subjects, thermal in 2, and tactile and olfactory in 1 subject each. Although the subject may assert that he is wide awake during the hypnagogic hallucination, this is not so, and electroencephalographic records show there is a loss of alpha rhythm at the time of the hallucination.

Hypnagogic hallucinations may be geometrical designs, abstract shapes, faces, figures, or scenes from nature. Auditory hallucinations of this kind may be animal noises, music, or voices. One of the commonest is that of the subject hearing his own name being called. Sometimes the voice says a sentence or phrase which has no discoverable meaning. In a subject deprived of sleep a hypnagogic state may occur, in which case there are hallucinatory voices, visual hallucinations, ideas of persecution, and no insight into the morbid phenomena. This condition usually disappears after the subject has had a good sleep.

c. Hallucinations of individual senses

i. *Hearing:* These may be elementary in the form of noises, or partly organized as music, or completely organized as hallucinatory voices. Elementary auditory hallucinations can occur in organic states and in schizophrenia. In the latter illness, they may form a part of the basis for the patient's delusion that he is the victim of some piece of machinery or apparatus which is spying on him, torturing him, or controlling his thoughts and actions.

Hallucinatory voices were called 'phonemes' by Wernicke in 1900. This term is less clumsy than the usual one, but it has the disadvantage that it is used as a technical term in linguistics for something quite different. 'Voices' are characteristic of schizophrenia and occur at some stage of the illness in most cases. They may, however, occur in organic states and, rarely, can be heard in severe depression.

Hallucinatory voices vary in quality, ranging from those which are quite clear, can be located in space and ascribed to specific individuals, down to those which are extremely vague and which the patients cannot describe in any way. It is noteworthy that patients are quite undisturbed by their inability to describe the direction from which the voices come and the sex of the person speaking. This is quite contrary to the experience of the normal individual. The voices give instructions to some patients, who may or who may not feel obliged to carry them out; this is the 'imperative hallucination'. In some cases the voices talk about the person in the third person and may even give a running commentary on his actions, which is very troublesome. They are usually abusive and often talk about sexual topics; thus female patients are called 'whores' and male patients 'homosexuals' and 'masturbators'. Occasionally the voices are friendly and reassuring and do not disturb the patient at all. At times the voices may speak incomprehensible nonsense or use neologisms.

The effect of the voices on the patient's general behaviour is variable. Quite a number of patients with continuous hallucinations are good workers in the mental hospital, but there are some patients in whom the voices are so insistent that they cut across all activity, so that the patient is dirty, dishevelled, and unable to look after himself or do any work. In other patients occupation with a mental or physical task diminishes the voices.

One special type which is characteristic of schizophrenia is the hearing of one's own thoughts being spoken aloud. There is no accepted English term for this symptom, which is known as *Gedankenlautwerden* in German and *echo de pensées* in French. Probably the best English term would be 'thought echo'. An alternative which is rather cumbersome is 'thought sonorization'. In acute schizophrenia quite a number of patients hear their thoughts being spoken as they think, and the voice which speaks their thoughts may come from inside or outside the head. In chronic schizophrenia the patient may complain that, as he thinks, other people in his environment are talking about his thoughts, so that his thoughts are being made known to other people. In this latter case it would appear that the patient is attributing his own thoughts to other people in the environment.

Patients explain the origin of the voices in different ways. They may insist that the voices are the result of witchcraft, telepathy, radio, television, atomic rays, and so on. Sometimes they claim that the voices come from within their bodies and may say that the voices come from within their arms, legs, chest, or stomach. Thus one patient heard the voices of two nurses and the Crown Prince of Germany coming from her chest. Some patients hallucinate speech movements and hear speech which comes from their own throats but has no connexion with their thinking. For example, one patient complained bitterly of her 'talky-talky tongue', because she was continuously auditorily hallucinated and felt speech movements in her tongue. It has, of course, been shown that subvocal speech movements occur in many normal subjects when they are thinking or reading silently, and it has also been shown by several investigators that patients hearing voices have slight movements of the lips, tongue, and laryngeal muscles and that there is an increase in the action potentials in the laryngeal muscles in these patients. It is, therefore, rather surprising that more schizophrenics do not complain of voices coming from their throats or tongues.

A few patients deny hearing voices but assert that people are talking about them. Careful investigation of the content and nature of the things which other people are alleged to have said shows that the patient has continuous voices and attributes them to real people in the environment.

As these are often abusive the patient may attack other patients, nurses, or doctors because of the abusive things they appear to be saying about him. A good example of this was a Greek patient who spoke little English and had been a patient in an English mental hospital for years. She always denied hearing voices and from time to time she made assaults on her fellow patients which appeared to be unmotivated. One day she was asked if she would like some Greek newspapers or visits from someone who spoke Greek. She said that this was not necessary because everyone in the hospital spoke pure Greek. It then became obvious that she heard continuous voices in Greek which she attributed to real people in her environment and that she attacked other patients who appeared to be saying abusive things about her.

ii. *Vision:* These may be elementary in the form of flashes of light, partly organized as patterns, or completely organized as visions of people, animals, or objects. Figures of living things and inanimate objects may appear against the normally perceived environment, or scenic hallucinations can occur in which whole scenes are hallucinated rather like a cinema film.

All varieties of visual hallucination are found in acute organic states, but small animals are most often hallucinated in delirium. For example, in delirium tremens patients usually see small animals such as rats, mice, squirrels, spiders, insects, and so on. Usually these hallucinations are associated with fear or even extreme terror. It has been claimed that negative scotomata occur in the visual fields of patients with delirium tremens and the hallucinations are due to a combination of peripheral and central disorders. Certainly these patients are extremely suggestible, so that one may persuade the patient with delirium tremens to read a blank sheet of paper. One investigator produced a disk of light by pressing on a patient's eyeball and persuaded him that he could see a dog. Scenic hallucinations are more common is psychiatric disorders associated with epilepsy. These patients may also have visions of fire and religious scenes such as the Crucifixion.

Often visual hallucinations are isolated and do not have any accompanying noises or voices. Sometimes, however, visual and auditory hallucinations form a coherent whole. Thus in temporal lobe epilepsy, patients may have combined auditory and visual hallucinations. For example, one of Penfield's patients had an attack in which he saw his workmates standing around him and they asked him for the number of a certain screw which he correctly said was No. 168593. Penfield stresses that these hallucinations in temporal lobe epilepsy appear to be vivid memories. He therefore calls them 'experiential hallucinations'. Chronic fantastic paraphrenics have scenic hallucinations in the form of mass hallucinations, when they see and hear people being murdered, mutilated, and tortured.

In some patients micropsia affects visual hallucinations, so that the patient sees tiny people, so-called Lilliputian hallucinations. Unlike the usual organic visual hallucinations these Lilliputian ones are usually accompanied by pleasure. For example, one patient with delirium tremens was very pleased when she saw a tiny German band playing on her counterpane.

Visual hallucinations are more common in acute organic states with clouding of consciousness than in the functional psychoses. The disturbance of consciousness makes it difficult for the patient to distinguish between mental images and perceptions, but there is some evidence to suggest that the delirious patient can sometimes distinguish between his hallucinations and real perceptions. Visual hallucinations are extremely rare in schizophrenia, so much so that they should raise doubt as to the diagnosis. Some schizophrenics describe 'visions' but these appear to be pseudo-hallucinations. Nevertheless, on occasion some of these patients insist that their hallucinations are substantial.

iii. *Smell:* Hallucinations of an odour can occur in schizophrenics, organic states, and, uncommonly, in depressives. It may, however, be difficult to be sure if there is a hallucination or an illusion. Thus there are some depressives who insist that they emit a smell and it is often difficult to know if they actually smell this odour, because it seems that they base their belief on the behaviour of other people, who, they say, wrinkle their noses or make underhand references to smells. Some schizophrenics insist that they can smell gas and that their enemies are poisoning them by pumping gas into the room. Temporal lobe attacks are often ushered in by an unpleasant odour, such as burning paint or rubber. At times the hallucination may occur without any fit, so that the patient then complains of a strange smell about the house. For example, one patient with a temporal lobe focus had no fits, but from time to time she would complain of a smell of stale cabbage water in the house and would turn the house upside down to find the offending object.

iv. *Taste:* Hallucinations of taste occur in schizophrenia and acute organic states, but it is not always easy to know whether the patient actually tastes something odd in his food, or if he feels so strangely changed that he can only explain his condition by assuming that he is being poisoned.

v. *Hallucinations of touch:* This usually takes the form of a feeling that animals are crawling over the body, so-called 'formication', and is not uncommon in acute organic states. In cocaine psychosis this type of hallucination nearly always occurs together with delusions of persecution and is known as the 'cocaine bug'. Some patients experience the feeling of cold winds blowing on them, sensations of heat, electrical sensations, and sexual sensations. The patient is firmly convinced that these sensations are produced by outside agencies, so that if they occur in the absence of coarse brain disease then the diagnosis is schizophrenia. Sexual hallucinations occur in acute and chronic schizophrenics, so that male patients complain that erections and orgasms are forced on them, and female patients that they are being raped and sexually abused. One patient seen by Professor Fish insisted that she could feel the penis of the son of her employer constantly in her vagina no matter what she did. She did not see the man, but she was certain that his penis was in her vagina.

vi. *Pain and deep sensation:* Twisting and tearing pains may be complained of by chronic schizophrenics. Sometimes the somatic hallucinations are described in a bizarre way, when the patient complains that his organs are torn out, the flesh ripped away from his body, and so on.

An interesting but unusual variety of somatic hallucinosis is delusional zoopathy. This may take the form of delusional infestation when the patient is convinced that there is an animal crawling about on his body. He does not see this animal but can usually describe it in detail. In some cases there is clearly an organic state. For example, Professor Fish had a patient with pellagra who believed that he was infested and was infesting everyone else. In other cases the patient appears to be schizophrenic. Two German authors reported a case of a man delusionally infested with an animal several centimetres long. The patient finally died after 7 years of illness and at post-mortem a tumour invading the thalamus was found. A variant of this condition is the patient who believes that there is an animal inside the body. For example, a patient had somatic sensations which she knew were the result of a wasp wandering around inside her body. This could be called 'internal delusional zoopathy' and the previous variety could be designated 'external delusional zoopathy'.

vii. *Vestibular sensations:* Sensations of flying through the air or sinking through the bed can be hallucinated. These are more likely to be found in acute organic states, most commonly in delirium tremens.

viii. *The sense of 'presence':* It is difficult to classify an abnormal sense of presence, because although it is not strictly a sense deception, it cannot be regarded as a delusion. Most normal people have from time to time the sense that someone is present when they are alone. Many people when in a dark street or climbing a dimly lit staircase on their own have the impression that there is someone behind them. Usually they dismiss this as ridiculous, but as a rule they look round to make certain. Some patients know that there is someone else present, whom they cannot see, and they may or may not know who this person is. For example, St. Teresa of Avila wrote: 'One day when I was at prayer—it was the feastday of the glorious St. Peter—I saw Christ at my side—or, to put it better, I was conscious of Him, for I saw nothing with the eyes of the body or the eyes of the soul. He seemed quite close to me, and I saw that it was He.' She says a little later: 'But I felt most clearly that He was all the time on my right, and was a witness of everything that I was doing.'

This experience was probably the result of lack of sleep and hunger and of religious enthusiasm. The hallucination of a presence can occur in organic states, schizophrenia, and hysteria.

d. Special kinds of hallucination

i. *Functional hallucinations:* A stimulus causes the hallucination, but it is experienced *as well as the hallucination.* For example, a schizophrenic patient first heard the voice of God talking to her as the clock ticked; later she heard voices coming from a running tap, and voices coming from the chirruping of the birds. She could hear both the noises and the voices; as she put it, 'God speaks to me through noise.' Some patients who discover that noises induce hallucinatory voices put plugs of cotton-wool in their ears to cut down the intensity of the hallucinations. This type of hallucination is not uncommon in chronic schizophrenia, but other patients with the same illness find that noise diminishes the intensity of their voices. This type of hallucination may be mistaken for an illusion by the unwary, but it is a hallucination because the provoking noise and the voices are both heard.

ii. *Reflex hallucinations:* This is a morbid variety of synaesthesia in which an image based on one sense modality is associated with an image based on another. In the reflex hallucination, a stimulus in one sensory field produces a hallucination in another. For example, a patient felt a pain in her head when she heard other patients sneeze and was convinced that the sneezing caused the pain.

iii. *Extracampine hallucinations:* The patient has a hallucination which is outside the limits of the sensory field. For example, he sees someone standing behind him when he is looking straight ahead, or he hears voices talking in London when he knows that he is in Liverpool. These hallucinations have no diagnostic significance; they can be hypnagogic, organic, or schizophrenic.

iv. *Autoscopy or the phantom mirror-image:* In this strange experience the patient sees himself and knows that it is he. It is not just a visual hallucination because kinaesthetic and somatic sensation must also be present to give the subject the impression that the hallucination is he. This symptom can occur in normal subjects, when they are depressed or very emotionally disturbed, and also tired and exhausted. In these cases there is some change in the state of consciousness. Occasionally autoscopy is a hysterical symptom. A few schizophrenics have autoscopic hallucinations, but they are more common in acute and subacute delirious states. The organic states which are most often associated with autoscopy are epilepsy and focal lesions affecting the parieto-occipital region and toxic infective states whose effect is greatest in the basal regions of the brain. The fact that autoscopy is often associated with disorders of the parietal lobe due to cerebrovascular disorders or severe infectious diseases accounts for the German folk-lore belief that when someone sees his double or *Doppelgänger* it indicates that he is about to die.

A few patients suffering from organic states look in the mirror and see no image. This is called 'negative autoscopy'. French psychiatrists have described internal autoscopy in which the subject sees his own internal organs. The description of the internal organs is that which would be expected from a layman acquainted with a butcher's shop. Internal autoscopy has not been reported in other countries.

e. *The patient's attitude to hallucinations*

In organic states the patient is usually terrified by the visual hallucinations and may try desperately to get away from them. Most delirious patients feel threatened and are generally suspicious. The combination of the persecuted attitude and the visual hallucinations may lead to resistance to all nursing care and to ill-considered attempts to escape from the threatening situation, so they may jump out of windows and jeopardize their lives. Usually patients with Lilliputian hallucinations enjoy them and may watch them with delight.

Depressed patients only hear disjointed voices abusing them or telling them to kill themselves. They are not terrified by these voices as they believe that they are wicked and deserve punishment. The instructions to kill themselves are not frightening, because they have thought of suicide for some time.

The onset of voices in acute schizophrenia is often terrifying. Later when the patient mistakenly finds the supposed source of the hallucinations he may be very angry and attack the people whom he holds responsible for them. He is often angry about the presence of the voices and their abusive content. Many chronic schizophrenics are not very troubled by the voices and may treat them as old friends, but a few patients complain bitterly about them and their persecution throughout the illness. Those patients in whom affect is better preserved may realize that it is considered abnormal to hear voices and therefore deny that they hear them. Usually the hearing of voices is obvious from their behaviour and their delusional beliefs. For example, in conversation with these patients, one can sometimes observe that they stop talking or listening, cock their heads, and turn their eyes sideways.

f. *The features of organic hallucinations*

By now it must be obvious that it is very difficult to discuss hallucinations in a consistent and logical way. For this reason a more extensive discussion of hallucinations in coarse brain disease is warranted. There is a tendency to stress the role of the focal lesion in organic hallucinations, but it must be remembered that they are total reactions of the brain and therefore also depend on the general condition of the brain, recent experiences, and psychodynamic factors as well as the effect of the local lesion.

In acute organic states such as delirium and organic hallucinosis there is an overall change in the brain, but so far the nature of this change and the way in which it causes hallucinations are unknown. Recently it has been shown that ditran, a very powerful anticholinergic substance, can produce typical delirium and subacute organic states.

Hallucinations produced by focal lesions are associated with a generalized change in the activity of the brain, which is shown clinically by a mild or moderate disorder of consciousness. Much of the work on hallucinations in focal disorders comes from the investigation of epileptics by Penfield and his group who studied spontaneous hallucinations and hallucinations produced by brain stimulation during operative investigation of temporal lobe epileptics. Unfortunately Penfield introduced his own terminology. He called hallucinations produced by epilepsy 'experiential hallucinations' and those produced by cortical stimulation 'experiential responses'. He used the word 'experiential' because these hallucinations were recognized by the subject as being past experiences. He also found that temporal lobe epileptics had interpretative signals or illusions, which were produced spontaneously or by stimulation. He divided these into auditory illusions, visual illusions, illusions of recognition, and illusional emotions. Auditory and visual illusions are sensory distortions, illusions of recognition are changes in familiarity of perceptions, and illusional emotions are ictal* emotions.

There is some evidence to suggest that recent experiences and psychodynamic factors influence the content of organic hallucinations in the same way as they influence that of dreams. However, in many cases the content of the hallucinations is very trivial and does not seem to be emotionally loaded.

i. *Visual hallucinations:* Eye disorders can cause visual hallucinations, but as has been already pointed out there is usually also a central disturbance as well. Stimulation of the visual projection area in the walls of the calcarine fissure causes the perception of flashes of light as does stimulation or irritation of the optic radiation. Lesions of the optic tract and the lateral geniculate bodies rarely case hallucinations. Spontaneous visual hallucinations are often associated with a sensory defect and it is rare for hallucinations to occur in a non-hemianopic field. Penfield found that stimulation of Brodmann's areas 17, 18, and 19 gave rise to coloured moving lights, stars, triangles, and zigzag lines reminiscent of scotomata in migraine. He also found that grey or black fog could be produced by the stimulation of these areas. Coloured objects were more commonly seen the nearer the site stimulated was to the occipital pole. Scenic complex hallucinations occurred following stimulation of the posterior part of the temporal lobe.

ii. *Tactile hallucinations:* These are almost exclusively the result of a lesion which produces a sensory defect. Disorders of the body image are most likely to occur in lesions of the parietal cortex or the adjacent subcortical areas. Stimulation of the parietal cortex causes paraesthesias and unpleasant sensations or the splitting off of the relevant region of the body.

---

* The word 'ictal' is used in the sense of a substitute for an epileptic attack.

Parietal lesions can distort the body image without causing any disturbance of sensation.

The phantom limb is the most common organic somatic hallucination. In this case the patient feels that he has a limb, from which in fact he is not receiving any sensations, either because the limb has been amputated or because the sensory pathways from it have been destroyed. In rare cases patients with thalamoparietal lesions have a phantom third arm or leg. In most phantom limbs the phenomenon is produced by peripheral and central disorders. Phantom limbs occur in about 95 per cent of all amputations after the age of 6 years. Occasionally a phantom limb develops after a lesion of the peripheral nerve or the medulla or spinal cord. The phantom limb does not necessarily correspond to the previous image of the limb. It may be shorter, or may consist only of the distal portion, so that, for example, the phantom hand arises from the shoulder. If there is some clouding of consciousness the patient may be convinced that the phantom limb is real. Some patients have very painful phantom limbs which can be difficult to treat.

iii. *Auditory hallucinations:* Whistling, buzzing, drumming and even bells can be heard by patients with middle or internal ear disease and also in the very rare cases of midbrain deafness. Hallucinations do not result from lesions between the medial corpora quadrigemina and the auditory cortex. Lesions of the thalamic projection to the auditory cortex can lead to sense distortions in the form of macracusia or acoustic quick motion.

Auditory hallucinations can be caused by epileptic foci and space-occupying lesions in the temporal lobes. Penfield produced auditory hallucinations by stimulating the first temporal convolution in areas 41 and 42 of Brodmann. The points were deep in the posterior third of the Sylvian fissure and were limited anteriorly by the central sulcus. The hallucinations which occurred were noises like the rushing of the wind, motor-cars, and railway trains. They were heard in the contralateral half of space or in both halves at the same time. Organized hallucinatory voices occurred on stimulation of the lateral surface of the first temporal convolution on both sides. The voices were associated with a sense of familiarity, so that Penfield called them 'experiential responses'.

iv. *Hallucinations of taste:* There is some doubt about the cortical projection area for taste. Adler claimed that it was in the insular cortex. Penfield produced hallucinations of taste by stimulating the depths of the Sylvian fissure around the transverse temporal gyri. Hallucinations of taste occur most often in temporal lobe epilepsy, when they are associated with salivation and chewing and sniffing movements.

v. *Olfactory hallucinations:* Hallucinations of smell are typical auras of temporal lobe epilepsy. Hallucinations resulting from lesions of the central pathway for smell have so far not been recorded.

vi. *Temporal lobe hallucinations:* These are multisensory hallucinations, but they do not include somatic sensations, which is to be expected because the somatic sensory area is separated from the temporal lobe by the Sylvian fissure. The temporal lobe contains the phylogenetically oldest parts of the brain and its neocortex lies between the occipital and frontal lobes. It has more extensive commissural connexions than any other part of the brain. The primary auditory field lies in this lobe as do parts of the cortical fields for smell and taste. The inferior and lateral portions of the temporal lobe belong to the allocortex and are connected with the mammillary bodies, the amygdaloid nuclei, and the posterior hypothalamic nuclei.

Penfield found that combined visual and auditory hallucinations occurred when the first temporal convolutions on both sides were stimulated, while visual hallucinations alone occurred on stimulation of a wide area of the lateral surface of the temporal lobe on the non-dominant side. On the dominant side, visual hallucinations followed stimulation of the lateral surface of the first and second temporal convolutions in 3 cases, while in 6 other cases stimulation of the superior surface of the first temporal convolution had this effect. This is because on the dominant side a large part of the posterior temporal lobe and the anterior portion of the occipital lobe are involved in the speech centre.

g. Hallucinatory syndromes

Schröder pointed out that hallucinations could occur in four main syndromes, which he called confusional, self-reference, verbal and fantastic.

i. *Confusional hallucinosis:* Here consciousness is clouded and visual hallucinations are prominent. Auditory hallucinations are mainly music, noises, or odd words, but connected sentences are occasionally heard.

ii. *Self-reference hallucinosis:* The patient hears voices talking about him. He can usually give only a rough idea of what the voices are saying and is unable to reproduce them word for word. The patient is convinced that the voices come from people in his environment and it may be difficult to decide if the patient is really experiencing hallucinations or is mishearing real conversations.

iii. *Verbal hallucinosis:* In this case the patient hears clear voices, which talk about him, and he can reproduce their content accurately. The voices may be attributed to real or imaginary people or to machines.

iv. *Fantastic hallucinosis:* Here hallucinations of all kinds seem to occur. The patient describes fantastic experiences which are based on auditory, bodily, and visual hallucinations. It is impossible to disentangle delusions and hallucinations. Sometimes it appears that the patient is describing dream experiences as if they were real. These patients usually have mass hallucinations in which they see and hear large numbers of people being murdered and tortured.

III. DISORDERS OF THE EXPERIENCE OF TIME

These disorders can be looked upon as distortions of perception and logically should have been discussed in the section on sensory distortions.

As this would have broken up the discussion of illusions and hallucinations it was decided to have a short note on this topic at the end of the chapter on perceptual disorders. From the psychopathological point of view there are two varieties of time, physical and personal. The first is determined by physical events, while the second is a personal judgement of the passage of time. We are all aware of the influence of mood on the experience of time. When we are happy 'time flies', but when we are sad it 'drags'. In severe depression the patient usually finds that time passes very slowly and if the depression is severe he may feel that time stands still. This arrest of time is often very dramatically expressed by patients with nihilistic delusions. Straus has claimed that the slowing down of time is characteristic of psychotic depression and does not occur in reactive depressive mood states. In contrast to the depressive the manic feels that time passes quickly. In acute schizophrenia personal time seems to go by fits and starts, so that some patients complain that the clocks are being interfered with. Sometimes the disorder of personal time in schizophrenia is the expression of the lack of continuity of self (*see* p. 79).

In acute organic states the disorder of personal time is clearly shown in the temporal disorientation. Patients with mild acute organic states without gross temporal disorientation may overestimate the progress of time. There is experimental evidence to show that hyperthermia is accompanied by an overestimation of time. Patients with post-encephalitic states may experience time as passing quickly or slowly during an oculogyric crisis. Some patients with temporal lobe lesions experience time as going too rapidly or too slowly.

Many earlier investigators found that the estimation of time by psychotics was not different from normal. In recent years Goldstone and Llamon and their associates have shown differences in time judgements of psychotics, They used auditory, visual, and tactile stimuli to mark off time intervals and began with an interval of 1·0 second. They increased and decreased the time interval in steps of 0·1 second in alternate series of measurements. The subject had to say when the time interval was more or less than 1 second. The time interval which was reported more or less than 1 second 50 per cent of the time was called the Second Estimation Point (S.E.P.). This was found to be lower in schizophrenics and depressives than in normals and to be higher than normals in manics. Using an estimation of the length of an interview lasting 30 minutes, Orme found that non-paranoid schizophrenics tended to underestimate the interview more than paranoid schizophrenics.

Chapter 4

Disorders of Thought and Speech

I. INTELLIGENCE

THIS can be roughly defined as the ability to think and act rationally and logically. In practice intelligence is measured by tests of the ability of the individual to solve problems and to form concepts by the use of words, numbers, other symbols, patterns, and non-verbal material. In most tests intelligence does not continue to develop after the age of 15 years, but the age at which intellectual growth ceases depends on the type of test used. In early adult life intelligence appears to be stable, but there is a slow decline which can be detected for the first time at about 35 years of age, after which there is a slow steady decline.

The best way of measuring intelligence is in terms of the distribution of scores in the population. Thus a person who has a 75 percentile has a score which is such that 75 per cent of the appropriate population score less and 25 per cent score more. Some intelligence tests used for children give a score in terms of the mental age, which is the score achieved by the average child of the corresponding chronological age. This is converted into an Intelligence Quotient by multiplying by 100 and then dividing by the chronological age of the individual, $I.Q. = 100 \times M.A./C.A.$ Since the growth of intelligence as measured by intelligence tests usually levels off at about 15 years of age, in the case of individuals over 15 years the I.Q. is obtained by using 15 as an arbitrary divisor. For historical reasons most intelligence tests are designed to give a mean I.Q. of the population of 100 with a standard deviation of 15. Even if the distribution of scores is not of Gaussian (normal) form, percentiles can be converted into standard units without difficulty, and this is probably the best way of measuring intelligence, although it is not yet in current use.

As pointed out before, intelligence scores in a group of normal subjects of the same age has a normal distribution, but this only applies over most of the range of scores. Towards the lower end of the range there is an increase in the incidence of low intelligence which is the result of brain damage caused by inherited disorders, birth trauma, infections and so on. There are therefore two groups of subjects with low intelligence or what is now called 'mental retardation'. The first group consists of subjects whose intelligence is at the lowest end of the normal range and is therefore a quantitative deviation from the normal. This has been called 'sub-

cultural mental defect' in the past. The other group of mental subnormality is the childhood psychiatric organic states. In the past the term
'amentia' has been used as a synonym for 'mental subnormality' because
the patient has never had a properly developed mind in contrast to the
dement who has suffered an intellectual deterioration. 'Amentia' is no
longer used in this sense, which is fortunate because it has also been used
by German-speaking psychiatrists to designate the subacute delirious
state.

Dementia is a loss of intelligence resulting from coarse brain disease.
Chronic schizophrenics to a greater or lesser degree lose their ability to
think logically and this has been called 'schizophrenic dementia'. The
present author prefers to restrict the term 'dementia' to intellectual decay
occurring as a result of coarse brain disease and to use the term 'schizophrenic deterioration' for the intellectual decline associated with chronic
schizophrenia.

II. THINKING

The verb 'to think' is used rather loosely in English. Leaving aside
such uses as 'to give an opinion' or 'to pay attention' there are three
legitimate uses of the word 'think'. These are:

1. Undirected fantasy thinking, which has been called 'autistic' or
'dereistic' thinking.

2. Imaginative thinking, which does not go beyond the rational and
the possible.

3. Rational thinking or conceptual thinking, which attempts to solve
a problem.

It is obvious that the boundaries between autistic and imaginative
thinking are not sharp as it may be difficult to decide where fantasy ends
and legitimate speculation begins. In the same way the boundary between
imaginative thinking and rational thinking is not sharp.

III. AUTISTIC THINKING

Autistic thinking is quite normal, but some quiet, shy people may
compensate for the disappointments of life by indulging in excessive
autistic thinking. Bleuler suggested that the schizoid individual became
schizophrenic when his autistic thinking became uncontrollable. He also
believed that excessive autistic thinking in schizophrenia was partly the
result of formal thought disorder. While the fantastic delusions of a few
chronic schizophrenics could be explained as the result of uncontrolled
autistic thinking, this explanation does not apply to all varieties of
schizophrenia.

IV. CLASSIFICATION OF DISORDERS OF THINKING

Any classification of these disorders is bound to be arbitrary. Thus it
has been customary to divide thought disorders into disorders of content

and disorders of form; or, to put it into more familiar language, disorders of belief and disorders of reasoning. It is obvious that this division is artificial because belief and reasoning cannot be sharply separated. Apart from these two disorders one can talk of disorders of the stream or progress of thought, which is also a somewhat arbitrary concept. Finally, there are disorders of the control of thinking, in which the subject is not in control of his thoughts, which may even be foreign to him. This might be considered as a disorder of volition or of ego-consciousness. Realizing that any division is bound to be arbitrary, it is suggested that for the sake of discussion we divide thought disorders into those of the stream of thought, the possession of thought, the content of thought, and the form of thought.

V. DISORDERS OF THE STREAM OF THOUGHT

These can be divided further into disorders of tempo and disorders of continuity.

1. Disorders of tempo

a. Flight of ideas

Here the thoughts follow each other rapidly, there is no general direction of thinking and the connexions between successive thoughts appear to be due to chance factors which, however, can usually be understood. The patient's speech is easily diverted to external stimuli and by internal superficial associations. The progress of thought can be compared to a game of dominoes in which one half of the first piece played determines one half of the next piece to be played. The absence of a determining tendency to thinking allows the associations of the train of thought to be determined by chance relationships, verbal associations of all kinds, such as assonance, alliteration, and so on, clang associations, proverbs, old saws, and clichés. The chance linkage of thoughts in flight of ideas is shown by the fact that one could completely reverse the sequence of the record of a flight of ideas and the progression of thought would be understood just as well.

An example of flight of ideas comes from a manic patient who was asked where she lived and she replied: 'Birmingham, Kingstanding; see the king he's standing, king, king, sing, sing, bird on the wing, wing, wing on the bird, bird, turd, turd.'

Flight of ideas is typical of mania. In hypomania so-called 'ordered flight of ideas' occurs in which, despite many irrelevances, the patient is able to return to the task in hand. In this condition clang and verbal associations are not so marked and the speed of emergence of thoughts is not as fast as in flight of ideas, so that this marginal variety of flight of ideas has been called 'prolixity'. Although these patients cannot keep accessory thoughts out of the main stream, they only lose the thread for a few moments and finally reach their goal. Unlike the tedious elaboration of details in circumstantiality, these patients have a lively embellishment of their thinking.

In acute mania, flight of ideas can become so severe that incoherence occurs, because before one thought is formulated into words another forces it way forward. Flight of ideas occasionally occurs in excited schizophrenics and in organic states, especially those resulting from lesions of the hypothalamus. In 1933 Foerster and Gagel pressed on the floor of the third ventricle of a patient who was being operated on under a local anaesthetic. This caused flight of ideas, pressure of speech, and elevation of mood, which stopped when the pressure was discontinued, but started again when it was reapplied.

What has been described so far as flight of ideas is really flight of ideas with pressure of speech. It has been claimed that flight of ideas without pressure of speech occurs in some mixed affective states.

b. Inhibition or retardation of thinking

The train of thought is slowed down and the number of ideas and mental images which present themselves is decreased. This is experienced by the patient as difficulty in making decisions, lack of concentration, and a loss of clarity of thinking. There is also a diminution in active attention, so that events are poorly registered. This leads the patient to complain of loss of memory and to the overvalued or delusional idea that he is going out of his mind. The lack of concentration and the general fuzziness in thinking are often associated with a strange indescribable sensation in the head, so that at times it is difficult to decide whether the patient is complaining about a physical or mental symptom. The poor intellectual performance in the retarded depressive may lead to a mistaken diagnosis of dementia.

Inhibition of thinking is typical of retarded depression, but is seen in the rare condition of manic stupor. Many depressives do not have inhibited thinking, but find it difficult to think because of their anxious preoccupations and the increased distractibility due to anxiety.

c. Circumstantiality

Here thinking proceeds slowly with many unnecessary trivial details but finally the point is reached. The goal of thought is never completely lost and thinking proceeds towards it by an intricate and devious path. This disorder has been explained as the result of a weakness of judgement and egocentricity. It is an outstanding feature of the epileptic personality change. Mild degrees of circumstantiality can be found in dullards who are trying to be impressive, and pedantic obsessional personalities.

2. Disorders of the continuity of thinking

a. Perseveration (*see also* p. 100)

Here mental operations tend to persist beyond the point at which the are relevant and thus prevent progress of thinking. Perseveration may be mainly verbal or ideational. Thus, a patient was asked in 1946 the name of the previous Prime Minister and replied, 'Churchill'. He was asked the name of the present Prime Minister and replied, 'Churchill. No, I mean Churchill'. This symptom is related to the severity of the task facing the patient, so that the more difficult the problem he is dealing with the more likely it is that perseveration will occur. Perseveration is common in generalized and localized brain disorders and, when present, can be considered to be almost pathognomonic. In the early stages, as in the above case, the patient can recognize his difficulty and tries to overcome it. It is clear that this is therefore not a problem of volition, which helps to differentiate it from verbal stereotypy which is a frequent spontaneous repetition of a word or phrase which is not in any way related to the current situation. In verbal stereotypy, the same word or phrase is used regardless of the situation, whereas in perseveration a word, phrase or idea persists beyond the point at which it is relevant.

b. Thought blocking

Here there is a sudden arrest of the train of thought, leaving a 'blank'. An entirely new thought may then begin. In patients who retain some insight, this may be a terrifying experience and this suggests that thought blocking differs from the experience that normal people have, of suddenly losing their train of thought, particularly when they are exhausted or very anxious. When thought blocking is clearly present it is a sign almost diagnostic of schizophrenia. However, it must be remembered that exhausted and anxious patients easily lose the thread of the conversation and may appear to block.

VI. DISORDERS OF THE POSSESSION OF THOUGHT

Normally the subject experiences his thinking as being his own although this sense of personal possession is never in the foreground of his consciousness. He also has the feeling that he is in control of his thinking. In some psychiatric illnesses there is a loss of control or sense of possession of thinking.

1. Obsessions and compulsions

The best definition of an obsession was given by Schneider as follows: 'An obsession occurs, when someone cannot get rid of a content of consciousness, although when it occurs he realises that it is senseless or at least that it is dominating and persisting without cause.' This definition is insufficient; one of the most important features of obsessions is that their content is of such a nature as to cause the sufferer great anxiety and even guilt. The thoughts are of such a nature that they are particularly repugnant to the individual; thus the prudish person is tormented by sexual thoughts, the religious person by blasphemous thoughts and the timid person by thoughts of torture, murder and general mayhem. It is of interest that the earlier writers emphasized the predominance of sexual obsessions whereas it would appear that nowadays the commonest form of obsession is concerned with fears of doing harm. Perhaps this reflects a social change: the Victorians were worried by sex, modern man is preoccupied with aggression. It is customary to distinguish between obsessions and compulsions. Compulsions are in fact merely obsessional motor acts. They may result from an obsessional impulse which leads directly to the action, or they may be mediated by an obsessional mental image or thought, as, for example, that the obsessional fear of contamination leads to compulsive washing.

The essential feature of the obsession is that it appears against the patient's will. It naturally follows that we can only call a mental event obsessional if it is normally under the control of the patient and can be resisted by the patient. Thus we can have obsessional mental images, ideas, fears and impulses, but not obsessional hallucinations, moods and perverse sexual drives.

Obsessional images are vivid images which occupy the patient's mind. At times they may be so vivid that they can be mistaken for pseudo-hallucinations. Thus one patient was obsessed by an image of his own gravestone, which clearly had his name engraved on it. Obsessional ideas take the form of ruminations on all kinds of topics ranging from why the sky is blue to the possibility of committing fellatio with God. Sometimes obsessional thinking takes the form of contrast thinking in which the patient is compelled to think the opposite of what is said. This can be compulsive blasphemy, as, for example, the devout patient who was compelled to make blasphemous rhymes, so that when the priest said 'God Almighty' she was compelled to think 'Sod Allshitey'. Obsessional impulses may be impulses to touch, count, or arrange objects, or impulses to commit antisocial acts. Apart from obsessions with suicide and homicide in depressed patients, it is very unusual for the obsessed patient to carry out an obsessive impulse. Obsessional fears or phobias consist of a groundless fear which the patient realizes is dominating without cause and must be distinguished from the hysterical and learned phobias.

Obsessions occur in obsessional states, depression, schizophrenia, and occasionally in organic states, particularly post-encephalitic states.

2. Thought alienation

While the obsessed patient recognizes that he is compelled to think about things against his will he does not regard the obsessional thoughts as being foreign and outside his control, i.e. he recognizes that they are his own thoughts. In thought alienation the patient has the experience that his thoughts are under the control of an outside agency or that others are participating in his thinking. In thought insertion he knows that thoughts are being inserted into his mind, and he recognizes them as being foreign and coming from without. In thought deprivation, the patient finds that as he is thinking his thoughts suddenly disappear and are withdrawn from his mind by a foreign influence. It has been suggested that this is the subjective experience of thought blocking and 'omission'. In thought broadcasting, the patient knows that as he is thinking everyone else is thinking in unison with him.

In all these experiences of thought alienation the general interpretation is that the boundary between the ego and surrounding world has broken down, so that it is not surprising that Schneider has claimed that these symptoms are diagnostic of schizophrenia.

VII. DISORDERS OF THE CONTENT OF THINKING

It is customary for most British textbooks to define 'delusion' more or less in the following way: 'A delusion is a false unshakeable belief, which is out of keeping with the patient's social and cultural background.' German psychiatrists tend to stress the morbid origin of the delusion, and quite rightly so. A delusion is the product of internal morbid processes and this is what makes it unamenable to external influences. The fact that it is false makes it easy to recognize but this is not its essential quality. A very common delusion among men is that their wives are unfaithful to them. In the nature of things, some of these wives will indeed have been unfaithful; the delusion will therefore be true, but only by coincidence. They also distinguish between true delusions and delusion-like ideas. True delusions are the result of a primary delusional experience which cannot be deduced from any other morbid phenomenon, while the delusion-like idea is secondary and can be understandably derived from some other morbid psychological phenomenon.

Another important variety of false belief, which can occur in normals and in the mentally ill, is the overvalued idea. This is a thought which, because of the associated feeling tone, takes precedence over all other ideas and maintains this precedence permanently or for a long period of time. If one takes the standard British textbook definition, it may at times be difficult to distinguish between the overvalued idea and a delusion. It is therefore more satisfactory to define delusions as false unshakeable beliefs of morbid origin, and to divide them into true delusions and delusion-like ideas.

1. Primary delusions

It is generally held that primary delusional experiences are diagnostic of schizophrenia, although similar experiences are occasionally met with in organic states, especially in epileptic psychoses. Delusion-like ideas, on the other hand, occur in all psychoses and in psychogenic reactions.

The essence of the primary delusional experience is that a new meaning arises in connexion with some other psychological event. Schneider has suggested that these experiences can be reduced to three, viz., delusional mood, delusional perception, and the sudden delusional idea. Since a new meaning is arising in connexion with some psychological event, Conrad suggested that the term 'apophany' would be a better term than 'primary delusional experience'.

In the delusional mood the patient has the knowledge that there is something going on around him which concerns him, but he does not know what it is. Usually the meaning of the delusional mood becomes obvious when a sudden delusional idea or a delusional perception occurs. In the sudden delusional idea a delusion appears fully formed in the patient's mind. This is sometimes known as an autochthonous delusion. The form of this symptom is not in itself diagnostic of schizophrenia, because sudden ideas or 'brain-waves' occur in normal and abnormal personalities. In depressive patients or in grossly abnormal personalities sudden ideas of the nature of delusion-like ideas or overvalued ideas can occur. If a patient has a very grandiose or bizarre sudden idea it is likely, however, that he is suffering from schizophrenia.

The delusional or apophanous perception is the attribution of a new meaning, usually in the sense of self-reference, to a normally perceived object. The new meaning cannot be understood as arising from the patient's affective state or previous attitudes. This last proviso is important because the delusional perception must not be confused with delusional misinterpretation. For example, a patient with delusions of persecution hears the stairs creak and knows that this is a detective spying on him. This is not a delusional perception, but a delusional misinterpretation. Schneider claims that delusional perception is diagnostic of schizophrenia and claims that the important feature of this symptom is its 'two memberedness'. He points out that there is a link from the perceived object to the subject's perception of this object and a second link to the new significance of this perception. Using this criterion, he has divided delusional memories into delusional perceptions and sudden delusional ideas. For example, if the patient says that he is of royal descent because he remembers that the spoon he used as a boy had a crown on it, this is really a delusional perception because there are the memory and also the delusional significance, i.e., there is 'two memberedness'. On the other hand, if the patient says that he is of royal descent because when he was taken to a military parade as a little boy the king saluted him, then this is a sudden delusional idea, because the delusion is contained within the memory and there is no 'two memberedness'.

Most of the older German psychiatrists held that the delusional perception was a disorder of thinking and that there was no change in perception. Matussek has challenged this assertion and pointed out that there are two kinds of delusional perception which we may call verbal and perceptual. An example of the verbal variety is the patient who was drying the dishes and had made a pile of plates. She picked up a plate, dried it, and put it down to make a fresh pile of plates. As the word 'pile' came into her mind it was followed immediately by the words 'pile of shit' and she took this experience to indicate that she was considered to be useless and worthless. This verbal indication of a delusional meaning is similar to some kinds of obsessional thinking in which words spoken or alluded to in the environment make the obsession worse.

In the perceptual variety of delusional perception the new meaning seems to be embedded in the perception itself. An example of this was an Englishman who was standing in a bar in a small town in New York State when his American brother-in-law picked up a long straight biscuit from the counter and said, 'Have one of these. They are salty'. Immediately the patient realized that his brother-in-law was accusing him of being a homosexual and was organizing a gang to spy on him.

Matussek has argued that perceptual changes occur in this variety of delusional perception, but so far no attempt has been made to correlate delusional perception and perceptual abnormalities in acute schizophrenia. Matussek has suggested that the essential properties of the perceived object come into prominence as a result of the loosening of the coherence of perception. The liberated essential property gives rise to the delusional meaning.

Primary delusional experiences occur in acute schizophrenic shifts and are not seen in chronic schizophrenia, where they have been buried under a mass of secondary delusions resulting from primary delusional experiences themselves, hallucination, formal thought disorder, and mood disorders.

2. Secondary delusions and systematization

Secondary delusions can, of course, be understood as arising from some other morbid experience. Some authors have tried to explain all delusions as a result of some other morbid phenomenon. Many have stressed the role of projection in the formation of delusions, but as projection occurs in the non-psychotic some other explanation is necessary to account for the excessive projection which occurs in delusions, particularly those of persecution.

Freud tried to explain delusions of persecution and grandeur as the result of latent homosexuality. The different ways in which this is denied gave rise to delusions of persecution, erotomania, jealousy and grandeur:

a. Delusions of persecution

The patient unconsciously thinks 'I love him—I do not love him—I hate him—he hates me.'

b. Delusions of love

Here the formula is: 'I love him—I do not love him—I love her.'

c. Delusions of jealousy

The denial takes the form 'I love him—I do not love him—she loves him.'

d. Delusions of grandeur

This arises as follows: 'I love him—I do not love him—I love no-one—I only love myself.'

These explanations are far fetched, but the idea that delusions of persecution, often incorrectly called 'paranoid delusions', are associated with ill-controlled latent homosexuality is an article of faith in Freudian psychopathology.

While most English-speaking psychiatrists accept the idea that delusions can be secondary to depressive moods and hallucinations, the idea that psychogenic reactions can give rise to delusion-like ideas is not well known. This leads many English-speaking psychiatrists to diagnose schizophrenia when confronted with firmly fixed delusions of jealousy or bodily ill health. In fact abnormally suspicious personalities can react to difficulties with delusion-like ideas of persecution or may slowly develop delusion-like ideas of marital infidelity or bodily ill health. These latter disorders can be regarded as abnormal personality developments.

Gaupp and his pupil Kretschmer tried to explain paranoid psychoses as understandable developments of sensitive personalities. By 'sensitive' Kretschmer meant that the person was sensitive about some psychological, social, or physical failing which he felt held him back from the success which was rightly his. This vulnerable point could be excessive masturbation, sexual perversion, illegitimacy, a physical defect, membership of a minority group, and so on. After years of struggle some key experience exposes the patient's weakness and he develops a full-blown paranoid psychosis. While there is no doubt that paranoid psychoses do occur in sensitive personalities they are not understandable developments of the personality. They are in fact either schizophrenia, endogenous depressions, or psychogenic reactions.

In schizophrenia once the primary delusional experiences have occurred they are usually integrated into some sort of system. This elaboration of delusions has been called 'delusional work'. It is still common in certain circles to divide delusions into systematized and non-systematized. In the completely systematized delusions there is one basic delusion and the remainder of the system is logically built on this error. In fact the present author has never seen a patient with completely systematized delusions. The more carefully one investigates a patient's delusions the more inconsistencies one finds, so that systematization is not a question of all or nothing, but of more or less.

Systematization appears to be related to the retention of integrity of the personality. When schizophrenia occurs in young persons it has a devastating effect on the integrity of the personality but this is very much less apparent in older patients. In the same way, incoherent and unintegrated delusions are common in young schizophrenics and much less so in older schizophrenics, where the delusions are customarily systematized more or less.

3. The content of delusions

The content of schizophrenic delusions is naturally dependent on the social and cultural background. Studies of old case records show that delusions have changed with the times. Kranz found that depressive delusions had not changed as much as schizophrenic ones, but Lenz found that delusions of guilt were less common in a series of depressed patients admitted to hospital in 1950 and 1955 than in one of patients admitted in 1925.

It is difficult to classify the content of delusions in any consistent way. They will, therefore, be discussed under the headings of delusions of persecution, jealousy, love, grandiosity, ill health, guilt, nihilism and poverty.

a. Delusions of persecution

We have already discussed the apophanous experiences which occur in acute schizophrenia and form the basis of delusions of persecution, but these delusions are also the result of auditory hallucinations, bodily hallucinations, and experiences of passivity.

Delusions of persecution can take many forms. In delusions of reference the patient knows that people are talking about him, slandering him, or spying on him. It may be difficult to be certain if the patient has delusions of self-reference or if he has self-reference hallucinosis. Ideas and delusions of reference are not confined to schizophrenia, but can occur in depressive illnesses and psychogenic reactions. Some severely depressed patients believe that they are extremely wicked, that other people know this and are therefore quite justifiably watching and spying on them. The delusions of guilt can be so marked that the patient believes that he is about to be put to death or imprisoned for life because of his wickedness. This alleged persecution is considered to be fully justified by the guilty depressive. However, one does rarely see depressives with ideas of reference and delusions of persecution who believe that the alleged persecution is not justified and may attribute their depression to it.

The supposed persecutors of the deluded patient may be definite people in the environment such as members of the family, neighbours, or former friends, or they may be organized groups such as Communists, Catholics, Freemasons, Jews, Capitalists, and so on. The group chosen naturally depends on the patient's background.

Some patients believe that they or their loved ones are about to be killed, or that they or their family are being tortured. In the latter case the delusions are based on somatic hallucinations. The belief that the family is be harmed may be deduced from the content of the hallucinatory voices or the patient may claim that his relatives have a strange look and are obviously suffering from some interference. It seems in these cases that there is some sort of perceptual change.

Some persecuted patients claim that they are being robbed or deprived

of their just inheritance, while others claim that they have special knowledge which their persecutors wish to take from them.

Delusions of being poisoned or infected are not uncommon. Some
morbidly jealous patients believe that the spouse is poisoning them. Often
delusions of poisoning are explanatory delusions. The patient feels
mentally and physically changed and the only way in which he can
account for this is by assuming that his food or cigarettes have been
poisoned. In other cases delusions of poisoning are based on hallucinations
of smell and taste.

Delusions of influence are a logical result of experiences of passivity
which are diagnostic of schizophrenia. These passivity feelings may be
explained by the patient as the result of hypnotism, demoniacal possession, witchcraft, radio waves, atomic rays and television.

It is customary for English-speaking psychiatrists to use the word
'paranoid' as a substitute for the term 'persecutory', but strictly speaking
the correct meaning is 'delusional'. 'Paranoia', which is the Greek for 'by
the side of the mind', was used in the late nineteenth century to designate
functional mental illnesses in which delusions were the most prominent
feature. The word 'paranoid' was derived from this term and naturally
had the meaning of 'like paranoia', or in other words 'delusional'. Despite
all the protests of the purists this word is now used by English-speaking
psychiatrists, psychologists, and social workers to mean 'persecutory',
'suspicious', or 'hostile'. It is also used in psychodynamic circles as a
term of abuse.

b. Delusions of jealousy

This term is a misnomer as the patient has morbid jealousy and
delusions of marital infidelity. These delusions may occur in organic and
functional conditions. Often the patient has been suspicious, sensitive,
and mildly jealous before the onset of the illness or psychogenic reaction.
Delusions of marital infidelity are not uncommon in schizophrenia and
have been reported in many different varieties of coarse brain disease,
but they are especially associated with alcohol addiction. Delusional
jealousy is also seen in the affective psychoses, but here again it is probably
a morbid exaggeration of a premorbid mildly jealous attitude.

Morbid jealousy is most troublesome in personality developments, in
which the suspicious insecure person becomes more and more convinced
of his wife's infidelity and finally the ideas reach delusional intensity.
The severity of the condition fluctuates in the course of time, so that
sometimes it seems to be a series of psychogenic reactions. During the
episodes of marked disturbance the spouse is interrogated unceasingly
and may be kept awake for hours at night. The jealous husband searches
his wife's underclothes for stains and claims that all stains are due to
semen. He usually says that his wife's vagina is moister than usual, that
she has bags under her eyes, and insists that these and other equally

ridiculous pieces of 'evidence' show clearly that his wife is having frequent sexual intercourse with someone else. Sometimes the wife is beaten or tortured to make her confess and not uncommonly murder is attempted or committed. Apart from the delusions of infidelity these patients have no other symptoms which would suggest schizophrenia. This condition conforms very well to Kraepelin's description of paranoia.

c. Delusions of love

This has also been called 'the fantasy lover' and 'erotomania'. The patient is convinced that some person is in love with them although the alleged lover may never have spoken to them. They may pester the victim with letters and unwanted attention of all kinds. If there is no response to their letters they claim that their letters are being intercepted, that others are maligning them to their lover, and so on. Occasionally isolated delusions of this kind are found in abnormal personality developments. Sometimes schizophrenia begins with a circumscribed delusion of a fantasy lover and in the course of a year or so the delusions become more diffuse and hallucinatory voices occur.

d. Grandiose delusions

The extent of the grandiosity varies. For example, some patients believe that they are God Almighty, Jesus, the Virgin Mary, the King of England and so on. Others are less expansive and believe that they are of the blood royal, great inventors, and so on. The expansive delusions may be supported by hallucinatory voices, which tell the patient that he is important, or they may be supported by confabulations, when, for example, the patient gives a detailed account of his coronation or of her marriage to the king. Grandiose and expansive delusions may be part of fantastic hallucinosis in which all forms of hallucination occur.

Delusions of grandeur have often been described as typical of general paresis, but although they appear to have occurred in about 50 per cent of general paretics in the middle of the nineteenth century, they seem to be less common today. General paresis is fairly rare in Britain today and usually presents as simple dementia or depression.

Delusions of grandeur occur in the happiness psychosis, when the patient believes that he is an important person and is able to help others. These patients often hear the voices of God and the saints. Although manic patients are often jocular in their manner and somewhat haughty, they do not usually have well-held expansive delusions. A good example of the expansive manic was a Jewish patient who said, 'I am Jesus Christ', and when asked what made him say that he replied, 'I am a Jew. Jesus Christ was a Jew. Therefore I am Jesus Christ.' He then roared with laughter.

e. Delusions of ill health

These are a characteristic feature of depressive illnesses, but are also found in schizophrenia and abnormal personality developments. Schneider has suggested that depressive delusions are the result of an uncovering of the patient's basic worries. Many people worry about their health, their finances, and their moral worth, so that when they become depressed they naturally develop delusions or overvalued ideas of ill health, poverty, or guilt. This explanation could be extended to cover persecutory delusions, because many people worry about their relationship with others and are suspicious of the intentions of other people. Such persons when depressed would be likely to develop overvalued ideas or delusions of persecution.

Depressives with hypochondriacal delusions believe that they have some incurable disease, such as cancer, tuberculosis, syphilis, a brain tumour, and so on. Delusions of syphilis or tuberculosis are not common in Britain today, probably because these diseases are much rarer than they were twenty years ago. Depressive delusions of ill health may involve the patient's spouse and children. Thus the depressed mother may believe that she has infected her children or that she is mad and her children have inherited incurable insanity. This may lead her to murder her children in the mistaken belief that she is putting them out of their misery. Many depressed puerperal women fear or believe that the newborn child is mentally subnormal.

Perhaps we might include in hypochondriacal delusions the overvalued ideas and delusions of incurable insanity. Quite a number of moderately depressed patients believe that they are becoming incurably insane. This may lead them to minimize their symptoms and refuse admission to psychiatric hospitals, because they believe that they will spend the remainder of their lives in an institution.

Hypochondriacal delusions in schizophrenia can be the result of a depressive mood, bodily hallucinations, and a sense of subjective change. In the early stages, these delusions are usually the result of depression and explanations of general psychological and physical inefficiency. In chronic schizophrenia they are usually the result of somatic hallucinations.

Chronic hypochondriasis may be the result of a personality development. The insecure bodily conscious person develops overvalued ideas of ill health which slowly increase in intensity and develop into delusions. Sometimes the delusions become obvious following an operation or a complication of drug treatment. Somewhat similar to these delusions are the delusional preoccupations with facial or bodily appearances, when the subject is convinced that his nose is too big, his face is twisted, or disfigured with acne, and so on. Sometimes these preoccupations with ill health or the appearance of the body have a somewhat obsessional quality, so that the patient cannot stop thinking about the supposed illness or deformity, although he realizes that it is ridiculous in times of quiet reflection. In other cases the belief is of delusional intensity and the patient is never able to admit that his belief is probably groundless.

f. Delusions of guilt

In mild cases of depression the patient may be somewhat self-reproachful and self-critical and it is considered that this serves to distinguish a true depressive illness from a reactive depression. In severe depressive illnesses self-reproach takes the form of delusions of guilt, when the patient believes that he is a wicked sinner and has ruined his family. He may claim to have committed an unpardonable sin and insist that he will rot in hell for this. The sin is usually masturbation or extra-marital sexual intercourse. In very severe depressions the delusions take on a somewhat grandiose character, and the patient may assert that he is the wickedest man in the world, the most terrible sinner who ever existed and that he will never die, but will be punished for all eternity. I remember an elderly woman, a missionary, who was in the throes of a retarded depression so severe that she was almost stuporose. I tried to find out why she felt so guilty and after much questioning she finally muttered almost in a whisper, 'I was there'. Clearly she was referring to the legend that all human souls were present at the Crucifixion and partook of the guilt thereof. These extravagant delusions of guilt are often associated with nihilistic ones. It has been already pointed out that delusions of guilt can give rise to delusions of persecution.

g. Nihilistic delusions

The French psychiatrists called these 'delusions of negation', because the patient denies the existence of his body, his mind, his loved ones, and the world around him. He may assert that he has no mind, no intelligence, or that his body or parts of it do not exist. He may deny his existence as a person, or that he is dead, the world has stopped, and everyone else is dead. These delusions occur in very severe agitated depressions, especially in so-called 'involutional melancholia'. Nihilistic delusions occasionally occur in subacute delirious states and in schizophrenia.

Sometimes nihilistic delusions are associated with delusions of enormity, when the patient believes that he can produce a catastrophe by some action. For example, he may refuse to pass water because he will flood the world.

h. Delusions of poverty

Here the patient is convinced that he is impoverished and believes that destitution is facing him and his family. These delusions are typical of depression, but they seem to be less common in Britain today than they were twenty-five years ago.

4. The reality of delusions

Although the deluded patient is convinced that his delusions are true, he does not necessarily act on them. The acute schizophrenic may attack or assault his alleged persecutors, but this does not commonly occur. Usually when the illness becomes chronic there is a discrepancy between the delusions and the patient's behaviour. For example, the grandiose patient may scrub the floor or the persecuted patient who insists that he is not ill remains in hospital as a voluntary patient.

Depressive delusions of guilt and hypochondriasis can lead to action if the patient is not retarded. Hypochondriacal delusions may lead to suicide or, if they affect the family, to homicide. Some guilty depressives try to give themselves up to the police.

Delusions or overvalued ideas of jealousy seem to be the most dangerous kind of delusion and overvalued idea. Thus East found that out of 200 sane murderers, i.e. not obviously psychotic, 46 had killed from motives of jealousy. It will be remembered that the most troublesome delusions of marital infidelity are the result of psychogenic reactions or personality developments and are therefore not true delusions.

It would seem therefore that action is more likely to be taken on the basis of delusion-like or overvalued ideas than on the basis of true delusions. This can easily be understood, because true delusions are the result of a disintegration of the personality, while overvalued ideas occur in an intact personality and delusion-like ideas can be present in non-schizophrenic illnesses without personality deterioration.

VIII. DISORDERS OF THE FORM OF THINKING

The term 'formal thought disorder' is a synonym for disorders of conceptual or abstract thinking which occur in schizophrenia and in coarse brain disease. While there have been many descriptions and investigations of schizophrenic formal thought disorder, there have been relatively few studies of conceptual thinking in coarse brain disease apart from studies of aphasia and psychological tests of brain damage. Cameron grouped the symptoms of disorganization resulting from functional or organic psychiatric states into incoordination, interpenetration, fragmentation, and overinclusion. He made no distinction between schizophrenic and organic disorders of conceptual thinking.

Let us leave the problem of organic formal thought disorder on one side and consider the schizophrenic variety. This can be divided into two subgroups, which can be called negative and positive. In the negative kind the patient has lost his previous ability to think, but does not produce any unusual concepts. It is, of course, not easy to decide if the patient's poor intellectual performance is the result of a rejecting attitude or if it is the result of a loss of ability to think logically. In positive formal thought disorder the patient produces false concepts by blending together incongruous elements.

Bleuler regarded schizophrenia as a disorder of association and pointed out that the outstanding feature of schizophrenic formal thought disorder was the lack of connexion between associations, which gave rise to changeable and unclear concepts. He believed that this incompleteness of ideas was the result of condensation, displacement, and the misuse of symbols. In condensation two ideas with something in common are blended into a false concept, while in displacement one idea is used for an associated idea. The faulty use of symbols consists in using the concrete aspects of the symbol instead of the symbolic meaning. Thus one of Bleuler's patients said, 'I hear a stork clapping in my body', by which she meant that she was pregnant. Bleuler borrowed the concepts of condensation, displacement, and the faulty use of symbols from Freud, who had pointed out that these mechanisms were characteristic of thinking in dreams.

Most other descriptions of schizophrenic formal thought disorder describe the same phenomena in terms of different psychological concepts, so that to describe them all would be tedious and repetitious. However, as the views of Cameron, Goldstein and Carl Schneider have led to some interesting research they will be discussed in some detail.

Cameron also stresses the lack of adequate connexions between successive thoughts and calls this 'asyndesis'. He points out that the patient uses clusters of more or less related thoughts in place of well-knit sequences and he is unable to eliminate unnecessary material and focus on the problem which he has to solve. The patient uses imprecise approximations in which some substitute term or phrase is used instead of a more exact one. Cameron calls these imprecise expressions 'metonyms' and points out that the patient develops his own private mode of speech which is full of personal idioms. It will be remembered that Cameron holds that interpenetration is one group of symptoms due to disorganization. Interpenetration in schizophrenic disorganization of thought takes the form of interpenetration of themes. The patient's speech contains elements which belong to the task in hand interspersed with a stream of fantasy which he cannot stop. Finally, Cameron claims that 'overinclusion' is an outstanding feature of formal thought disorder. This is an inability to maintain the boundaries of the problem and to restrict operations within their correct limits. The patient cannot narrow down the operations of thinking and bring into action the relevant organized attitudes and specific responses. The schizophrenic is therefore able to generalize and shift from one hypothesis to another, but his generalizations are too involved, too inclusive, and too much entangled with private fantasy.

Goldstein claimed that in schizophrenia and in coarse brain disease there was a loss of the abstract attitude, so that thinking became concrete, i.e. the patient was unable to free himself from the superficial concrete aspects of thinking. Goldstein held that the difference between the concrete thinking in coarse brain disease and schizophrenia was that in the latter condition the patient had not lost his fund of words.

The concepts of overinclusion and concrete thinking have been used by many investigators. Payne has claimed that tests of concrete thinking which are performed badly by schizophrenics with formal thought disorder are in fact tests of overinclusion. Payne found that not all schizophrenics showed overinclusion, and those who did not, tended to show marked psychomotor slowness. Starting with the concept of overinclusion Chapman has carried out a large number of interesting investigations of schizophrenic formal thought disorder. She has shown that there is evidence to suggest that one disorder in schizophrenic conceptual thinking is that the schizophrenic cannot free himself from the major meaning of a word.

Schneider claimed that five features of formal thought disorder could be isolated, viz. derailment, substitution, omission, fusion and drivelling. In derailment the thought slides on to a subsidiary thought, while in substitution a major thought is substituted by a subsidiary one. Omission consists in the senseless omission of a thought or part of it. In fusion heterogeneous elements of thought are interwoven with each other, while in drivelling there is a disordered intermixture of constituent parts of one complex thought. Schneider suggested that there were three features of healthy thinking, which were:

1. *Constancy:* This is the characteristic persistence of a completed thought whether or not it is simple or complicated in its content.

2. *Organization:* The contents of thought are related to each other in consciousness and do not blend with each other, but are separated in an organized way.

3. *Continuity:* There is a continuity of the sense continuum, so that even the most heterogeneous subsidiary thoughts, sudden ideas, or observations which emerge are arranged in order in the whole content of consciousness.

Schneider claimed that schizophrenics complained of three different disorders of thinking which correspond to these three features of normal thinking. These were:

1. A peculiar transitoriness of thinking.

2. The lack of normal organization of thought.

3. Desultory thinking.

There were three corresponding varieties of objective thought disorder, viz. transitoriness, drivelling and desultory thinking.

1. *Transitory thinking*

Here derailments, substitutions and omissions occur. Omission is to be distinguished from desultory thinking because in desultoriness the continuity is loosened but in omission the intention itself is interrupted and there is a gap. The grammatical and syntactical structure are both disturbed in transitory thinking.

2. *Drivelling thinking*

The patient has a preliminary outline of a complicated thought with all its necessary particulars, but he loses his preliminary organization of the thought, so that all the constituent parts get muddled together. The patient with drivelling has a critical attitude towards his thoughts, but they are not organized and the inner material relationships between them become obscured and change in significance.

3. *Desultory thinking*

Speech is grammatically and syntactically correct, but sudden ideas force their way in from time to time. Each one of these ideas is a simple thought which if used at the right time would be quite suitable.

Schneider claimed that there were three symptom groups in schizophrenia which could occur separately or in combinations. These three different types of thought disorder correspond to his three symptom groups, which he called 'desultory', 'thought withdrawal', and 'drivelling'. In the desultory group affective blunting, lack of drive, somatic hallucinations, and desultory thinking are the outstanding features. Although there is a general decrease in the intensity of emotions, states of exaltation alternating with ill-humoured mood states occur. The thought withdrawal group is characterized by transitory thinking, thought withdrawal, delusional inspiration, experience of passivity, religious and cosmic experiences, and perplexity. The main features in the drivelling group are primary delusional experiences, loss of interest in things and values, inadequate affective responses, and drivelling thinking. While Schneider held that various combinations of these symptom groups usually occurred, Astrup has claimed that they occur in relatively pure form in acute schizophrenia. He found that the desultory syndrome could occur either in a hebephrenic-paranoid clinical picture or in a catatonic one. The thought withdrawal syndrome was found in paranoid schizophrenia with projection symptoms, while the drivelling syndrome occurred in paranoid schizophrenia with systematized delusions.

IX. SPEECH DISORDERS

Aphasia or dysphasia is a disorder of speech resulting from interference with the functioning of certain areas of the brain. Some psychiatrists, particularly Kleist and his pupils, have described speech disorders in schizophrenia and compared them with aphasia. However, as Critchley has pointed out, there are considerable linguistic differences between the verbal productions of aphasics and schizophrenics. Despite certain disadvantages, speech disorders will be grouped into functional and organic for purposes of discussion. Some functional speech disorders which are found in catatonic schizophrenia are basically special examples of catatonic motor disorders. These will be discussed in more detail in the section on psychotic disorders of speech in the chapter on motor disorders.

1. Speech disorders which are mainly functional

a. Stammering and stuttering

In stammering the normal flow of speech is interrupted by pauses or by the repetition of fragments of the word. Grimacing and tic-like movements of the body are often associated with the stammer. This disorder usually begins about the age of 4 and is much more common in boys than in girls. Often it improves with time and only becomes noticeable when the patient is anxious for any reason. Sometimes it persists into adult life when it may be a very severe social handicap. Occasionally stammering occurs during a severe adolescent crisis or at the onset of an acute schizophrenia. This is probably the result of severe anxiety bringing to light a childhood stammer which has been successfully overcome.

b. Mutism

This is the complete loss of speech and may occur in disturbed children, hysteria, depression, schizophrenia, and coarse brain disease. Elective mutism occurs in children, who refuse to speak to certain people. As a rule the child is mute at school but speaks when at home, but sometimes he speaks to some relatives and not to others. In some abnormal families refusal to speak is a recognized technique of dealing with family quarrels. Occasionally one finds families in which some members of the family have not spoken to others for years although they live under the same roof and meet at meals. Hysterical mutism is fairly rare and the commonest hysterical disorder of speech is aphonia. Depressive stupor may be associated with mutism, but more often there is poverty of speech and the patient replies to questions in a slow painful way. Mutism is nearly always present in catatonic stupor (*q.v.*), but it may occur in non-stuporose catatonics as a mannerism. Thus in 1935 a catatonic patient said, 'My words are too valuable to be given away' and thereafter she never spoke a word. When she was seen 20 years later she was still mute, but she would make her wants known by gesture and at times would write the answers to questions when given a pencil and paper. Although the use of words is very restricted in severe motor aphasia, complete mutism does not occur, because the patient may use one or more verbal stereotypies and may use expletives under emotional stress. In pure word dumbness the patient is mute, but he can and will read and write. In akinetic mutism which is associated with lesions at the base of the brain there is mutism, and the patient appears to be aware of his environment. These patients have a lowering of the level of consciousness and antero-grade amnesia.

c. Talking past the point. Vorbeireden

In this disorder the content of the patient's replies to questions shows that he understands what has been asked and is deliberately talking about an associated topic. For example if asked, 'What is the colour of grass?' the patient may reply, 'White', and then when asked, 'What colour is snow?' he may reply, 'Green'. One patient when asked the year when the First World War began gave her year of birth, and when asked for the year of her birth replied '1914'. *Vorbeireden* occurs in hysterical pseudodementia when mental symptoms are 'unconsciously' being presented for some advantage. Often pseudodementia is really malingering, so it is preferable to refer to it as the 'Ganser syndrome' or 'Ganserism'. It was first described by Ganser in criminals awaiting trial for serious offences. Sometimes *Vorbeireden* is found in acute schizophrenia. The patient is usually adolescent and finds the effect of his *Vorbeireden* amusing. This indicates a silly facetious attitude and can be regarded as a hebephrenic symptom. Conrad called this syndrome 'pseudo-pseudo-dementia'. A few chronic catatonics talk past the point, particularly when they are asked personal questions which they find painful, such as the length of their stay in hospital. They seem to say the first thing which comes into their heads. These patients will always reply to a question no matter how ridiculous it is.

d. Neologisms

These are new words which are constructed by the patient or ordinary words which he uses in a special way. The term 'neologism' is usually applied to new word formations produced by schizophrenics. Some aphasic patients, particularly those with motor aphasia, use the wrong word, invent new words, or distort the phonetic structure of words. This is usually known as 'paraphasia' although superficially the words resemble neologisms. Kleist claimed that some schizophrenic neologisms could be regarded as the result of paraphasia, but this view is not generally accepted. When the schizophrenic produces a new word it may be completely new and its derivation cannot be understood; it may be a distortion of another word, or it may be a word which has been incorrectly constructed by the faulty use of the accepted rules of word formation.

Neologisms in catatonics may be mannerisms or stereotypies (*q.v.*). The patient may distort the pronunciation of some words in the same way as he distorts some movements of his body. Some patients use a stock word instead of the correct one. Thus one of Kleist's patients used the word 'vessel' and called a watch a 'clock vessel' and a lamp a 'light vessel'. In other cases neologisms appear to be a result of severe positive formal thought disorder, so that words are fused together in the same way as concepts are blended with one another, or the neologism may be the obvious result of a derailment, e.g. a patient used the word 'relativity' instead of the word 'relationship'. In other cases the neologism seems to be an attempt to find a word for an experience which is completely outside the realms of normal. This can be called a technical neologism, because the patient is making up a technical term for a private experience which cannot be expressed in ordinary words. In other patients hallucinatory voices seem to play a great part in the formation of neologisms.

The 'voices' may use neologisms and this may lead the patient to use them as well. Sometimes the patient feels forced to use new words in order to placate the 'voices' or to protect himself from them.

Malapropisms, which are ludicrously misused words, are not of psychiatric significance, except that they may be used by bewildered dullards and mistaken for neologisms.

e. Speech confusion and schizophasia

In a few chronic schizophrenics speech is utterly confused. These patients talk utter nonsense and yet some of them are able to carry out fairly responsible work which does not involve the use of words. Since the disorder of speech is so prominent in these patients Bleuler called this type of schizophrenia 'schizophasia'. There is, of course, a superficial resemblance to aphasia where the disorder of speech is much greater than the defect in intelligence. Despite this apparent discrepancy between thought and speech most psychiatrists regard schizophasia as a variety of thought disorder. Schizophasia has also been called 'speech confusion' and 'word salad'.

2. Aphasia

This brief discussion of aphasia has been included in order that the functional disorders of speech can be compared with the organic. It is not intended to be exhaustive. The reader interested in a detailed treatment of this topic should consult the standard neurological textbooks, particularly *Speech Disorders—Aphasia, Apraxia and Agnosia*, by Lord Brain (1966).

In right-handed subjects speech is controlled by the posterior part of the first temporal convolution and the adjacent parts of the parietal and occipital lobes. In order to avoid repetition in the subsequent discussion when the site of the lesion usually associated with a type of aphasia is given, it will be assumed that the patient is right-handed.

Crude perception occurs when incoming impulses in the sensory tracts activate the specific cortical area for the given sense modality, but complete perception of an object does not occur until the association area is activated. A perceived object is named when the word schema for the object emerges as a result of the activation of the speech centre. Thus a written or spoken word cannot be understood if the visual or auditory cortical areas respectively are isolated from the speech centre. Brain has put forward the view that the recognition of words depends on an organized neuronal pattern which he has called the 'schema'. This schema automatically calculates the probability that a certain set of properties are to be found in a given pattern of neuronal activity. Brain also suggests that there are motor schemas which excite the cells of the precentral cortex to produce the correct pattern of motor activity needed to pronounce the word. Speech takes place when incoming sensory information is relayed to the speech centre and brings into action preliminary schemas for words, which in turn cause a pattern of signals which pass to the motor speech area in the posterior part of the third frontal convolution. Here motor schemas are activated which give rise to a pattern of impulses passing to the motor area. This in turn causes activation of the appropriate fibres in the motor tracts which bring into action the lower motor neurons controlling the muscles involved in speech. In aphasia the input, the central organization, or the output of the cortical speech mechanisms may be disordered, so that we may classify aphasia into receptive, intermediate or expressive.

a. Receptive aphasias

Three types of aphasia can be regarded as receptive: they are 'pure word deafness', 'agnosic alexia' and 'visual asymbolia'. In pure word deafness the patient hears words, but cannot understand them, so that his native language sounds foreign to him. This usually results from a lesion near the left first transverse temporal gyrus. This gyrus is the primary auditory cortex, so that the interruption of its connexions with the speech centre prevents the activation of auditory word schemas. A lesion which affects the connexions between the visual cortex on both sides and the speech centre causes agnosic alexia in which the patient can see but cannot read words. In right-handed subjects the lesion is in the left angular gyrus which receives connexions from both the right and the left visual cortical areas. In visual asymbolia or cortical visual aphasia there is also a lesion in the left angular gyrus which is extensive enough to affect the posterior part of the speech centre. This leads to a disorganization of visual word schemas, so that words cannot be recognized and motor word schemas cannot be activated. The patient, therefore, finds it difficult to read and write. As the lesion may be extensive and affect neighbouring structures, this variety of aphasia is often associated with other neurological disorders such as inability to use mathematical symbols (acalculia), spatial disorientation, visual agnosia, nominal aphasia, and right homonymous hemianopia. Patients with visual asymbolia are often able to understand words or sentences which they cannot read aloud or which they read aloud incorrectly. Unlike patients with agnosic alexia they can copy writing to some extent but have difficulty in writing spontaneously.

The agnosias are related to the receptive aphasias. In these disorders the patient experiences sensation in a given sense modality but he cannot recognize objects. Thus in visual agnosia the patient can see but cannot recognize what he sees, although he can recognize objects if he feels them. As Brain has pointed out, patients with agnosia can neither describe nor use the object so that there is both an aphasia and an apraxia. A detailed discussion of agnosia is not possible, but it should be remembered that this condition may be mistakenly regarded as hysterical if it occurs in isolation. Thus one patient with visual agnosia said that he could not see although he was obviously not blind. He was therefore diagnosed incorrectly as suffering from hysterical amblyopia.

b. Intermediate aphasias

Nominal (amnestic) aphasia and central aphasia are varieties of intermediate aphasia due to lesions affecting the speech centre. The nominal aphasic cannot name objects although he has plenty of words at his disposal. Usually he finds it difficult to carry out verbal and written commands and he cannot write spontaneously, although as a rule he can copy written material. Difficulty in finding the correct word can occur in other varieties of aphasia, but in nominal aphasia it is the outstanding disorder. It usually results from a lesion in the left temporoparietal region.

In central aphasia the patient cannot understand written and spoken words and the grammatical relationships between words. Speech is faulty in grammar and syntax and there is paraphasia. Both the receptive and expressive aspects of speech are affected. This type of aphasia has also been called 'receptive aphasia', 'cortical sensory aphasia', and 'syntactical aphasia'. It is usually the result of a lesion of the posterior part of the first left temporal convolution.

c. Expressive aphasias

The main type of expressive aphasia is cortical motor aphasia, which is also known as Broca's aphasia, verbal aphasia, or expressive aphasia. It is usually caused by lesions of Broca's area, the motor speech centre, which is in the posterior two-thirds of the third frontal convolution, but it can result from lesions affecting the association fibres which run forward from the speech centre in the first temporal convolution. In this type of aphasia the patient has difficulty in putting his thoughts into words, and in severe cases speech may be restricted to expletives and a few words. The patient may use only one word, a paraphasic word, a phrase, or either 'yes' or 'no' or both these words. Frequently if a phrase is used it was present in the patient's mind when the lesion occurred. Jackson called these repeated phrases 'recurring utterances', but they could be called 'verbal stereotypies'. Often these recurring utterances are produced with a different intonation to communicate different meanings. When the disorder is less severe the patient understands what is said to him and knows what he wants to say but cannot find the right words. Words are often mispronounced and those with several syllables tend to be abbreviated. As a rule the patient realizes that he is making mistakes and tries to correct them. Although words are often omitted, the organization of sentences is not as severely affected as the use of words. The omission of particles and short words gives rise to what has been called 'the telegram style'. Serial responses are often not affected so that the patient may be able to count, recite the alphabet, and give the days of the week. The expressive quality of speech is disordered so that the intonation and stress are unusual and speech sounds stilted and odd. Usually the patient can swear and say words under emotional stress. Thus one of Jackson's patients shouted, 'Fire!' when she saw a fire in the street through the ward window.

In pure word dumbness the patient is unable to speak spontaneously, to repeat words and to read aloud, but he can write spontaneously, copy, and write to dictation. This disorder was called 'subcortical motor aphasia', because it was assumed that the connexions between the motor speech area and the motor cortex were interrupted. In fact it occurs in vascular and traumatic lesions affecting extensive areas of the frontal lobe, the insula, and anterior parts of the temporal lobe.

Chapter 5

Disorders of Memory

I. GENERAL INTRODUCTION

FOLLOWING Welford we can isolate seven stages in memory. These are:
1. Adequate perception, comprehension, and response to the material to be learned.
2. A short-term storage mechanism.
3. Formation of a durable trace.
4. Consolidation in which traces are often modified or simplified by subsequent learning.
5. Recognition that certain material needs to be recalled.
6. Isolation of the relevant memory.
7. Recalled material is used in new situations.

In the discussion of memory disorders we shall see that disturbances can occur at one or more of these stages. For purposes of discussion we can divide memory disorders into amnesias and dysmnesias, i.e. into loss of memory and distortion of memory.

II. THE AMNESIAS

These can be divided into psychogenic and organic. Much nonsense is talked about psychogenic 'forgetting', some of it by psychiatrists who prefer to study books rather than patients, and some of it by those to whom it is a repeated act of faith. We forget things for many reasons, but time fades all memories unless they are refreshed by recall. The following are standard acceptable statements; this does not mean that they are true.

1. Psychogenic amnesias

Undue anxiety will interfere with perception and comprehension leading to lack of memory; complexes may prevent recall; and a mental conflict may be resolved with amnesia. We therefore have anxiety amnesia, katathymic amnesia, and hysterical amnesia.

a. Anxiety amnesia

This may occur in psychogenic reactions or in morbid anxiety, particularly in depressive illnesses. In psychogenic reactions the loss of memory due to anxious preoccupation may suggest the symptom of amnesia as a hysterical solution of the patient's problems.

b. Katathymic amnesia

The subject has a set of ideas which are disturbing when conscious. They are therefore repressed in an attempt to avoid the affect which they would otherwise produce. This is therefore a complex-determined partial amnesia. This may occur in normals, but it is more frequent and extensive in hysterics.

c. Hysterical or dissociative amnesia

Here there is complete loss of memory and loss of identity, but the patient can carry out complicated patterns of behaviour and is able to look after himself, so that there is a gross discrepancy between the marked memory loss and the intact personality. By the time the patient with coarse brain disease has total amnesia he is quite unable to look after himself in any way. Hysterical amnesia is often associated with a fugue or wandering state. As pointed out above, the symptom of amnesia may be suggested by the amnesic effect of anxiety. It may also be suggested to the patient by the memory of amnesia following a head injury in the past.

Some hysterical amnesics are trying to escape from the consequences of their criminal activities. Amnesia is not uncommonly the response of an embezzler to the threat of discovery of his crime. Stories of patients losing their memories completely and adopting a new personality are doubtful to say the least. Many of the older textbooks cite the story of the Reverend Ansel Bourne who disappeared from his home in Providence, U.S.A., and two months later came to himself in Norristown, 200 miles away, where he was working as a shopkeeper. The last thing that he did before leaving Providence was to draw a large sum of money from his bank. The loss of memory and the assumption of a new identity are best regarded as a cover story of a man who was deliberately escaping from some difficulty, which resolved itself in the two months while he was away. Perhaps a pregnant Sunday School teacher had aborted in the meantime.

I have met a few cases of hysterical amnesia. I have never been able to convince myself that there was any truth in their statements about their alleged loss of memory.

2. Organic amnesias

a. Acute coarse brain disease

In these conditions memory is poor owing to disorders of perception and attention and also because of the failure to make a permanent trace.

In acute head injury there is an amnesia which embraces the events just before the injury. This is known as 'retrograde amnesia' and covers a period at most of a few minutes before the injury. Both Schilder and Gillespie showed that hypnosis or intravenous barbiturates will bring back a large number of memories for events just before the head injury. In subacute conditions, such as the amnestic state, the patient may have a retrograde amnesia which stretches back over a period of years before the onset of the disease. This is due to destruction of memory traces, whereas the retrograde amnesia of head injury is the result of disturbance of the short-term memory.

It used to be held that the extent of the retrograde amnesia in head injury was of prognostic significance. It has, however, been shown that the severity of a head injury is directly related to the duration of post-traumatic amnesia. This amnesia is, of course, the interval between loss of consciousness and the appearance of full awareness and memory.

Anterograde amnesia is the result of a failure to make permanent traces and occurs in many acute organic states, in which the patient is apparently fully conscious but has no memory for the events which occur. For example, a boxer is struck heavily on the chin and continues fighting, but he has no memory of the fight after the blow. A similar amnesia occurs in the alcoholic 'blackout' which occurs after the subject has a few 'short' drinks. He loses his memory for a period, during which he is not drunk. In most acute psychiatric organic states there is some degree of amnesia. The delirious patient usually has only a fragmentary memory of his illness. In organic twilight states due to epilepsy or alcohol (pathological drunkenness) there is often a complete loss of memory. The patient may commit some atrocious crime and not appear confused or drunk.

b. Subacute coarse brain disease

The characteristic memory disorder here is the amnestic state, in which the patient is unable to register new memories. Apart from this there is disorientation for place and time, euphoria, and confabulation. Wernicke called registration of new memories 'impressibility', and some German authors have claimed that in some patients with the amnestic syndrome there is a complete loss of impressibility. Although the amnestic patient has difficulty in acquiring new memories, tests of recognition show that these patients are indeed able to acquire them, but have difficulty in recall. It seems as if there are three faults, viz. difficulty in forming permanent traces, difficulty in recall, and thought disorder. The disorder of thinking is an inability to change set. Once thought is proceeding in a given direction it continues in that direction for an unnecessarily long time and instead of being corrected by incoming information it distorts this information. This 'tram-line' thinking distorts the material that does get registered and makes recall difficult.

c. Chronic coarse brain disease

The amnestic or Korsakoff patient usually has a loss of memory extending back into the recent past for a year or so. The patient with a progressive chronic brain disease has an amnesia extending over many years. In dementing illnesses the memory for recent events is lost before the memory for remote events. This was first pointed out by Ribot and is known as Ribot's law of memory regression.

III. DISTORTION OF MEMORIES

These can be conveniently divided into disorders of recall and recognition.

1. Disorders of recall

Inaccuracy of recall can be designated as 'paramnesia' and may take the form of retrospective falsification. retrospective delusions, delusional memories, and confabulations.

a. Retrospective falsification

The subject modifies his memories in terms of his general attitudes. We all falsify the past to some degree. Nietzsche put the matter very well when he wrote: 'I have done that—says my memory; I could not have done that—says my pride and remains inexorable. Finally the memory gives in.' Nevertheless, although this may be good philosophy or literature, it is bad psychology. Memory and pride cannot be regarded as two persons engaged in an argument. In normal people the degree of retrospective falsification is inversely related to the degree of insight and self-criticism of the individual. The hysterical personality can therefore produce a complete falsified set of memories of the past.

Excessive retrospective falsification is common in depressive illnesses. The patient looks back over the past and sees only his failures. He overlooks the fact that he has become ill only in the recent past and insists that he has always been a useless worthless person. This may give the impression that the patient has always been an inadequate unstable person. It might perhaps be better to say that the memories are not so much falsified as revalued.

Memory falsification resulting from mood and lack of insight may occur in agitated depression and mania. Patients who have recovered from these illnesses may remember all the restrictions which were placed on them, but forget the justification for these measures. Thus many manics after an attack of mania insist that they were unjustly detained in hospital and harshly treated for no reason. They gloss over their overactive, troublesome, interfering excited behaviour.

b. Retrospective delusions

Some schizophrenics back-date their delusions. For example, the patient may insist that he has been persecuted for many years despite the fact that there is clear evidence that his illness is of recent origin. This could be regarded as delusional retrospective falsification, because fragments of true events are interwoven with the delusional reminiscences.

c. Delusional memories

As has been pointed out elsewhere, primary delusional experiences may take the form of memories, and Schneider has divided these delusional memories into sudden delusional ideas and delusional perceptions.

d. Confabulations

This is a detailed false description of an event, which is alleged to have occurred in the past. Some authors, such as Bleuler, insisted that a confabulation was not only a detailed false memory, but also could be influenced by the examiner, because patients with true confabulations were suggestible. For Bleuler, confabulations were characteristic of organic states. Nevertheless, hysterical psychopaths and some chronic schizophrenics produce detailed false memories which for the want of a better word must be called 'confabulations'.

The pathological liar is an hysterical personality who obtains the appreciation which he needs by telling lies. Minor varieties of this are quite common and many people grossly exaggerate and falsify the past in order to impress other people. This might be called 'the fish that got away' syndrome. Some individuals with an odd sense of humour tell fantastic lies as a joke and enjoy the effect that they have on naïve listeners. The original Baron Munchausen did this, but unfortunately Raspe, a German psychopath, when short of money while in London embellished a few of the Baron's stories and added a few old facetiae and published them as *The Surprising Adventures of Baron Munchausen*. Asher has used the term 'Munchausen syndrome' for those hysterical psychopaths who haunt hospitals with bogus illnesses, fantastic medical histories, and often one or more operation scars. These patients are merely one variety of pathological liar and are often quite dishonest in other ways. Some hysterical psychopaths enjoy dressing up in uniforms and posing as officers in the Armed Forces, while others pass themselves off as secret service agents. As many secret service agents are immature histrionic individuals it may be difficult to distinguish these patients from the real thing until one learns the facts about their activities.

The pathological liar can be regarded as a person with a vivid fantasy life and extreme suggestibility which leads him to confuse fantasy with reality. Given the right circumstances a convincing pathological liar can become a confidence trickster. When faced with incontrovertible evidence these individuals will usually admit they are lying. In view of this, some authors prefer to say that these patients have pseudo-reminiscences rather than confabulations.

Confabulation always occurs in the amnestic syndrome, but it is not necessarily a presenting symptom. Patients with this syndrome can often be persuaded to confabulate by asking a question which is likely to lead to a false answer, for example asking a patient who has been in hospital for some days if she went shopping the day before. It has been suggested that the Korsakoff patient confabulates in order to fill in the gaps in his memory. The mechanism of confabulation could be explained as a result of the 'tram-line' thinking. If, for example, the patient is asked what he has done the day before, some reminiscences will come into his mind and the tram-line thinking will begin to construct a detailed memory out of a few reminiscences which are probably quite false. Conrad has shown that some amnestic patients will construct completely false explanations of TAT cards based on one false interpretation of a detail. The incorrigibility of the confabulation can of course be explained as an effect of the increased suggestibility of these patients.

Some schizophrenics confabulate, producing detailed descriptions of fantastic events which have never happened. These patients produce the most ridiculous fantastic memories without turning a hair. These confabulations may support the patient's claim to the throne and so on. Leonhard suggests that these patients have a special type of formal thought disorder which he calls 'pictorial thinking'. Bleuler objected to the use of the term 'confabulation' in these cases, because the memories are fixed and unchangeable. He preferred to call them 'memory hallucinations', which does not seem to be a very suitable term.

It is difficult to decide if the 'hallucinatory flashbacks' which occur in temporal lobe epilepsy spontaneously or during brain stimulation should be considered as disorders of memory. As they have the quality of perceptions they have been discussed in the section on hallucinations. These phenomena would merit the designation 'memory hallucination' more than the confabulations in chronic schizophrenia.

2. Distortions of recognition

a. Déjà vu and déjà vécu

Here the subject has the feeling that he has seen or experienced the current situation before. The sense of recognition in *déjà vu* is never absolute, so that misidentification does not occur. These experiences occur occasionally in normals but they may become excessive in temporal lobe lesions. *Déjà vu* usually ushers in the typical temporal lobe attack.

b. Misidentification

This may occur in confusion psychosis and in acute and chronic schizophrenia. It may be positive when the patient recognizes strangers as his friends and relatives. In confusional states and acute schizophrenia at most a few people are positively misidentified. However, some chronic schizophrenics give a false identity to every fresh person whom they meet. In negative misidentification the patient denies that his friends and relatives are the people whom they say they are and insists that they are strangers in disguise.

Some patients assert that some or all of the people whom they meet are doubles of real people. In the so-called 'Capgras syndrome' the patient insists that every person whom he meets is a double of the person whom he claims to be. In Greek mythology the God Zeus took the form of Amphitryon and his servant took the form of Amphitryon's servant Sosias. Zeus did this in order to have sexual intercourse with Alcmene, Amphitryon's wife. In keeping with this legend, patients who believe that their spouses are doubles can be said to be suffering from the 'Amphitryon illusion', while those who believe that other people as well as the spouse are doubles have the 'Sosias illusion'. The commonest cause of the Capgras syndrome is schizophrenia, but it occasionally occurs in very hysterical women who feel that they are being rejected by their husbands and families.

In acute schizophrenia misidentification can be based on a delusional perception. The subtle change in the perception associated with the emergence of a new meaning may lead the patient to misidentify people.

Leonhard has suggested that negative misidentification could result from an excessive concretization of memory images, so that the patient retains all the minute details of the characteristics of the people whom he encounters. When he sees the same person again he compares the new perception with the exact memory image. Since there are bound to be a few minor discrepancies between the memory image and the perception, the patient fastens on these and asserts that it is not the same person.

Chapter 6

Disorders of Emotion

I. DEFINITIONS

It is customary to distinguish between feelings and emotions. A feeling can be defined as a positive or negative reaction to some experience. It can also be regarded as the subjective experience of emotion. Unfortunately the word is also in common use as a synonym of 'presentiment' and 'belief'. An emotion is a stirred-up state due to physiological changes which occurs as a response to some event and which tends to maintain or abolish the causative event. There is evidence to suggest that there is not a specific pattern of physiological changes for each separate emotion, but that the emotion is designated by the content of consciousness which has evoked the physiological changes. Affects are waves of emotion in which there is a sudden exacerbation of emotion usually as a response to some event. Some psychiatrists have divided affects into sthenic and asthenic varieties. The sthenic affects are anger, rage, hate or joy, and the asthenic are anxiety, horror, shame, grief and sadness. This division seems to be based more on the content of the emotion than on the physiological changes or perhaps a need to invent classifications. Affectivity has been used to designate the total emotional life of the individual. It is common to call those severe illnesses in which the primary disorder is one of mood 'affective psychoses'. It is difficult to see why these terms 'affect' and 'affectivity' should continue to be used as they merely mean 'short-lived emotion' and 'emotional life' respectively.

Strictly speaking, mood is the emotional state prevailing at any given time or, as Deese puts it, 'the dominant hedonic tone of the moment'. However, mood is often used by psychiatrists for an emotional state which usually lasts for some time and which colours the total experience of the subject. Strictly speaking this should be called 'a mood state'. Thus while an emotion is a short-lived response, a mood state is a lasting disposition, either reactive or endogenous, to react to events with a certain kind of emotion.

II. THE CLASSIFICATION OF EMOTIONAL DISORDERS

Some emotional reactions are normal responses of the sick person to a primary morbid psychological experience. Thus a normal person would become fearful if he were subjected to such assaults on the coherence of his mental life as thought insertion, experiences of passivity, and terrifying hallucinations. These understandable secondary emotional states will not be discussed any further.

As has been pointed out already, we use the term 'abnormal' in the sense of 'morbid' or of 'a quantitative deviation from the mean'. Thus when we speak of 'abnormal emotions' we can mean either an excessive emotional response or an emotional state resulting from a morbid process in the nervous system. In the following discussion the word 'abnormal' will be used for excessive responses of a normal kind and the word 'morbid' for those phenomena which appear to be the result of a morbid process, within the nervous system. We can, therefore, classify emotional disorders into:

1. Abnormal emotional predispositions.
2. Abnormal emotional reactions.
3. Abnormal expressions of emotion.
4. Morbid disorders of emotion.
5. Morbid disorders of the expression of emotion.

1. Abnormal emotional predisposition

These are to be found in abnormal personalities, as, for example, the hyperthymic personality where the person is overcheerful and is not touched by the minor irritations of life. Such individuals often have short periods of gloom in which they resemble the dysthymic personality who always looks on the sad side of life and is miserable. Some psychiatrists consider that these abnormal temperaments are constitutionally determined, by which they probably mean genetically caused. This may be true of the hyperthymic, dysthymic, cyclothymic, and irritable temperaments which are often found in patients with manic-depressive disease. Other predispositions to emotional disorders are probably partly, if not wholly, determined by childhood experiences. Some subjects have an increased emotional responsiveness, so that their mood swings from euphoria to depression with slight changes of their emotional environment. Disinhibited behaviour easily occurs in such individuals and they are often highly suggestible. The reverse kind of temperament is seen in the emotionally cold personality, who has a general indifference, lack of emotion, and an absence of finer feelings. It has been suggested that maternal deprivation gives rise to affectionless individuals. In some cases it does seem that these emotionally callous people have prolonged unpleasant childhood experiences which may have determined their emotional poverty, but as similar experiences can be found in other subjects without this kind of temperament, it seems probable that there is also some constitutional predisposition as well. These affectless individuals may at times be mistaken for schizophrenics because of their emotional indifference. However, unlike the hebephrenic schizophrenic whom they resemble, they have always had a poor emotional response and there has been no recent change in their emotional expression.

In children and adolescents there is normally a lack of constancy in emotional feeling and instinctual life. This is usually associated with a lack of persistence, a tendency to egotism, cruelty, outbursts of emotion, and overvalued thinking. Usually this instability disappears with maturity but may last into the third or fourth decade and occasionally throughout life.

When children grow into the stage of adolescence, they leave the social niche of childhood and enter into the adult world of freedoms and responsibilities. They desire the freedoms but do not understand the responsibilities or how to cope with them. They are eager to assert their adulthood and therefore come into conflict with those, especially parents, who are only too acutely aware of their inexperience. In consequence, there is inevitably some degree of conflict. The result is internal insecurity and ambivalent attitudes towards other people. Some degree of ambivalence is normal because we all have positive and negative feelings towards the people we know or meet. Usually the positive or negative feeling greatly exceeds the opposite one and only the dominant feeling is conscious. If the positive and negative feelings are more evenly balanced then slight changes may reverse them. This leads the adolescent to swing rapidly between positive and negative attitudes to the same person or thing. As the disturbed adolescent has markedly ambivalent attitudes towards his parents and parent substitutes, his relationships with them tend to be very stormy.

2. Abnormal emotional reactions

The normal person is able to withstand the effects of external stimuli and preserve an emotional balance, but each person has his breaking-point. The type of emotional disturbance which occurs depends naturally on the subject's personality and on the traumatic situation. The commonest reaction is that of anxiety or, more correctly, fear. English-speaking psychiatrists tend to call exaggerated states of normal fear 'acute anxiety states'. Anxiety is an unpleasant affective state with the expectation, but not the certainty of something untoward happening. A definition which is briefer and to the point is 'a fear for no adequate reason'. The psychiatrist is, therefore, using the term 'anxiety' in a somewhat different sense from its day-to-day use which is 'an uneasy preoccupation with some personal matter' or 'worrying about something'. This leads many English-speaking patients to deny that they are anxious. Quite often the reply to the question 'Do you feel anxious?' is 'No, doctor, I have nothing to be anxious about.' These patients, however, will often admit that they feel frightened for no reason. Anxiety is often associated with an increase in tone in the voluntary muscles, so that the patient has a sense of tension and complains of feeling tense. Some anxious patients are not aware of the relation between the cause of their anxiety and their symptoms. They present therefore with physical complaints which they do not connect with their life problems. When fear becomes intense chaotic motor behaviour may occur which is usually called 'panic'. Overwhelming frightening experiences may lead to fear which paralyses the subject, so that he becomes stuporose, or it may lead to ill-directed overactivity which may lead the subject into even graver danger.

Phobias are fears restricted to one object, situation, or idea. In some cases they are obviously learned, when, for example, the girl learns to be afraid of mice from her mother, or the child is frightened by a dog or other animal and then has a phobia of dogs or animals. Some phobias such as the fear of going out alone seem to be hysterical in that they are unconsciously used to obtain some advantage but this certainly does not apply to the majority of 'agoraphobics'. Other phobias are obsessions (q.v.), and dominate the mind without reason.

The emotional reaction to chronic frustration and disappointment is depression. It is often assumed that depression following a bereavement or loss of some kind is merely quantitatively different from the mood state which occurs in so-called 'endogenous depression'. For example, Foulds writes: 'There seems little reason to regard the intensity of the melancholic's depression as any greater than the intensity of the grief felt by countless normal people on the death of someone they greatly loved.' Although at times it is difficult to distinguish between exaggerations of normal depression and morbid depression, in typical cases there are clear differences which are described by the intelligent patient. It is unfortunate that the same word has to be used for the normal reaction to disappointment and for the morbid or pathological mood which occurs in depressive illness. Even worse, the word depression is also used to mean the syndrome of 'depressive illness'. The whole subject of depression is bedevilled by words which are either misused or which have no clear meaning. For example, depressive illness is commonly classified into 'reactive' or 'endogenous', signifying that the illness has been precipitated by psychological stress or not. In practice these words are used to refer to syndromes or patterns of symptoms. The term 'reactive depression' is also used to mean the normal reaction by an individual following a bereavement. In consequence, it is almost impossible for two psychiatrists to engage in a discussion on the depressions which does not end in confusion and incoherence.

Morbid depressed mood in the mildest forms is difficult to distinguish from the experience of depression produced by disappointment or loss. In its severer forms it reaches an intensity which only the sufferer can appreciate. It is accompanied by feelings of helplessness and hopelessness, morbid preoccupations and loss of judgement. It is also associated with other symptoms all of which indicate a fundamental psycho-physiological disturbance. The syndrome of depressive illness can be precipitated by psychological stress but it can appear equally for no ascertainable reason.

There are some hyper-reactive individuals who respond to stress not only with depressed mood but with many other disabling symptoms. These constitute one of the forms of 'reactive depression'. It is said that they are usually not self-reproachful but tend to blame others for their illness. Morbid thinking is not present, threats of suicide are not infrequent, and even suicidal attempts though these are not often serious threats to life. Often anger and resentment are ill-controlled, so that with a judicious and sympathetic approach on the part of the examiner the patient's anger becomes obvious. Loss of weight, loss of interest and loss of libido, the typical symptoms of true depressive illness, are not common but sleep is almost invariably disturbed.

There is unfortunately no English equivalent for the German term *Verstimmung* which is best translated as 'ill-humoured mood state'. These irritable, angry depressive states are often called 'moodiness' in everyday speech, but most English-speaking psychiatrists call them 'depressions'. However, unlike the ordinary depressive these patients are not only unhappy themselves, but make others unhappy as a result of their unpleasant, aggressive behaviour. Mood states of this kind are seen particularly in disturbed adolescents and certain types of abnormal personality, particularly those called 'psychopaths' by English-speaking psychiatrists. It will, however, be obvious that the borderline between a reactive depressive mood state and an ill-humoured state is not well marked.

Euphoria, which is best defined as undue cheerfulness and elation, is not usually reactive. The hyperthymic individual is usually euphoric, while the cyclothymic, dysthymic, and irritable personalities have episodes of euphoria which are not morbid. Euphoria may occur as a result of some unexpected good fortune, but this does not become marked enough to be considered abnormal.

3. Abnormal expressions of emotion

By definition this means persons who show emotional expression and behaviour very different from the average normal reaction, but not different in kind. Excessive emotional response may be the result of learning (different cultures have different norms) or it may be subsumed under the term 'emotional lability', but inadequate response is of greater interest and importance. The commonest and most important is a lack of manifestation of anxiety or fear under conditions where this would be expected. This is often referred to as 'dissociation of affect' and is said to be an unconscious defence reaction against anxiety. As almost every symptom of mental disorder has been said to be a defence against anxiety, this does not explain much. In any case, the term covers a number of different forms of behaviour.

The first is plain denial of anxiety. The terrified adolescent who has got himself into severe trouble may put on a bold front and pretend that he is not afraid; he is 'brazening it out'. Nevertheless, he does experience anxiety or fear and he is aware of it, whatever he may say. Similar to this is the situation of, for example, a group of soldiers under bombardment. However much afraid each man may be he will make every endeavour to cover it up. This is not only because once fear starts its spread may lead to panic, thereby increasing the soldiers' danger, but also because the fear of being regarded with contempt by others can be greater than the fear of death. Mankind is, after all, a social animal.

Another variant of dissociation of affect is the *belle indifférence* of the conversion hysteric. In the older literature we can read of hysterics with gross symptoms and severe disabilities who yet were undisturbed by their suffering. Gross hysterics of this type are very rare nowadays and they usually have a bland air of patient martyrdom, not the sort of thing that would be called indifference by a modern psychiatrist.

Under conditions of great stress and anxiety, it is quite common for individuals to find themselves momentarily preoccupied with minute aspects of their situation. This could be regarded as a defence mechanism, did it not also occur under conditions of great pleasure, happiness or joy.

The most extreme example of dissociation of affect is the description given by the explorer David Livingstone of the feeling he had when he was siezed by a lion: 'It caused a sense of dreaminess in which there was no sense of pain nor feeling of terror, though I was quite conscious of all that was happening.' It would appear that he was describing what is known as 'derealization'.

Dissociation of affect should not be applied to the emotional indifference that is often found in violent criminals, who are usually able to discuss their unpleasant crimes without any emotion. It may be that they were callous to begin with, but in any case human beings can become used to anything. Dissociation of affect should not be applied to apathy which is strictly speaking a loss of all feeling. Apathy is often used to mean emotional indifference and a lack of activity, often associated with a sense of futility. This combination of symptoms is found in some subjects who have a traumatic depersonalization, do not attempt to escape from danger and are completely indifferent to their fate. In prisons, concentration camps, depressed areas, and other situations of hopelessness apathy is common, but as well as the psychological causes it may be partly due to a chronic organic state resulting from malnutrition.

It is difficult to decide on the subgroup of emotional disorders into which perplexity should be placed. Perhaps it is best considered as an abnormal expression of emotion. It is of course a state of puzzled bewilderment which can occur in anxiety, mild clouding of consciousness, and acute schizophrenia, when new strange psychotic experiences are occurring. Leonhard claims that perplexed stupor is characteristic of the inhibited phase of the confusion psychosis.

4. Morbid disorders of emotion

The most outstanding disorder of this kind is the depressed mood state, which occurs in manic-depressive and endogenous depressions. The morbid sadness in this condition may be associated with morbid thinking which may reach delusional intensity. The delusions in morbid depression have already been discussed (*see* p. 46). Often there is inhibition of thinking, loss of drive, and decreased voluntary activity. There may also be difficulty in making decisions, inner unrest, loss of self-confidence, anxiety, and lack of pleasure in living. As Hamlet put it:

> How weary, stale, flat, and unprofitable
> Seem to me all the uses of this world.

All experiences are considered from the worst aspect and everything is seen in a gloomy light. Only troubling thoughts, often with the same content, spontaneously come into the mind, so that the patient is constantly preoccupied by unpleasant thoughts and has difficulty in concentrating on the task in hand. Normal activity is carried out with a sense of difficulty and incompetence against a background of inner emptiness and desolation. The patient often complains of a muzziness in the head which seems to be an attempt to express the difficulty in thinking. Often the patient feels a tight band around his head. German psychiatrists have stressed the occurrence of 'precordial anxiety' in morbid depression. This is a sense of oppression in the chest associated with anxiety, and has led Schneider to use the term 'vital hypochondriacal' depression for this type of depression.

Morbid depression also abolishes the normal reactive changes of emotion or emotional resonance. This leads to a sense of inner emptiness or deadness, so that the patient does not feel that he is participating in the world any more. This loss of feeling for the environment gives the depressive the impression of unreality. This loss of emotional resonance gives rise to complaints of depersonalization and derealization in morbid depressions but is obviously not at all the same. Possibly this mechanism is partly responsible for depersonalization in schizophrenia, but here the symptom appears to result more from the subjective experience of the breakdown of the boundaries of the self, which finally becomes obvious in apophanous experiences, passivity feelings, and thought alienation.

Morbid depression is usually associated with diurnal variation, loss of energy, loss of libido, anorexia and early morning waking. If the depression is severe and inhibition is marked, stupor may occur. The apparent indifference of the severe morbid depression must be differentiated from an irreversible emotional devastation of schizophrenia. The severe depressive is able to understand ethical values and adopt a moral attitude, but he is unable to act accordingly and he experiences his failure to do so as something painful and reprehensible. For example, the house-proud woman realizes that her house is not being run according to her high standards and this makes her very unhappy and extremely self-critical.

Apart from manic-depressive disease and endogenous depressions, morbid depressions are found in schizophrenia and in acute and chronic organic states, in particular cerebral arteriosclerosis, epilepsy, and general paresis.

Morbid anxiety often occurs in association with morbid depression and gives rise to the clinical picture of agitated depression. There is, however, no one-to-one relationship between the inner feeling of anxiety and the degree of agitation. Thus some extremely anxious depressives are almost mute and stuporose, because their intense anxiety paralyses all voluntary action. Morbid anxiety is also found in organic states. Most delirious patients are anxious and fearful and many are frankly terrified, especially by the visual hallucinations. They often believe that doctors, nurses, and other attendants are conspiring against them and they are therefore very frightened. Mild acute and chronic coarse brain disease often produces mild anxiety mixed with depression and irritability, which has been called 'organic neurasthenia'.

Anxiety or fear is not uncommon in paranoid schizophrenia, but it is difficult to regard it as morbid, since it can be understood as a natural reaction to the delusions and hallucinations.

Ill-humoured states may be seen in morbid depression, schizophrenia, and organic states. In depression they are often the expression of an abnormal personality, but they are occasionally the result of a mixed affective state, in which there is a manic element in addition to the depression. Although the manic patient is usually cheerful and elated, ill-humoured manic states occur, in which the patient is irritable, querulous, and awkward. These irritable manics make unjustified complaints of interference and persecution. Sometimes the complete manic phase is of this kind, while in other cases the patient may pass into an ill-humoured state for a short time and then pass back into classic mania or hypomania.

Irritability may occur in any organic state, but it is rarely seen in the amnestic syndrome. Ill-humoured states are very common in epilepsy, when the patient becomes truculent, awkward, and physically or verbally aggressive. These states may occur when there have been no fits for some time and they often improve after the patient has a fit. Sometimes when the fits are well controlled by medication the patient is ill-humoured and his mental state improves when his epilepsy becomes less well controlled.

Some patients with temporal lobe foci have ictal moods which last for a few minutes or less. These are short-lived states of depression, anxiety, euphoria, or extremely unpleasant feelings.

The acute schizophrenic may describe his frightful experiences with an indifferent air as if he were talking about trivial matters. Chronic schizophrenics may behave in the same way but in addition they have no drive, no interest in anything, are difficult to employ, and hang about the mental hospital or day hospital completely indifferent to their lot. Leonhard has called this type of schizophrenia 'apathetic hebephrenia'. Sometimes depressives are described as being 'apathetic'. This is really an enforced indolence resulting from psychomotor retardation or severe anxiety. The patient has a general sense of insufficiency and is unable to get going. He may also 'feel that he has no feeling', because of the loss of emotional resonance. Strictly speaking, this anergic state is not apathy because the patient is not completely indifferent, it is rather that he is too preoccupied with his miseries. Chronic organic states, particularly those in which the frontal lobes are affected, may be associated with apathy.

Morbid euphoria and elation classically occur in mania, but they are seen in organic states and occasionally in schizophrenia. In mania there is a jovial mood which is completely unmotivated. There is a general sense of well-being with cheerful thoughts and a lack of response to depressing influences, so that everything is seen in the best possible light. In hypomania the mental illness may be obvious only to the relatives and doctors, and other outside observers may merely regard the patient as a cheerful chap or somewhat of a 'card'. The elated mood state leads to faulty judgement and a lack of consideration for others. There is a general overactivity and disinhibited behaviour. Hypersexuality may lead to venereal disease in men and pregnancy in women. Poor judgement and excessive drive may lead to swindling, immoral behaviour, and other crimes which may bring the patient in conflict with the law.

In hypomania there is an increased pressure of speech with prolixity, an abnormal liveliness of expressive movements, superficial bustling activity, and a tendency to be argumentative and irritable if thwarted in any way. The patient is interested in everything, starts many projects, and finishes none. In mania the excitement is more marked and flight of ideas is present. The patient is usually very distractible and his overactivity may lead to exhaustion. In most cases of mania or hypomania there is an infectious gaiety which leads the examiner to underestimate the morbid nature of the mood.

In the elation which occurs in general paresis and other organic states and in schizophrenia there is a silly cheerfulness and flight of ideas is rarely present. Some hebephrenics have a silly cheerfulness which is often associated with spiteful and annoying behaviour. Some chronic paraphrenics are elated and bring forth fantastic and expansive delusions with enthusiasm. The expansive general paretic is elated, but he also is somewhat childish and has boastful grandiose delusions and no true flight of ideas. The manic, on the other hand, does not have well-held grandiose delusions. Lesions of the hypothalamus may produce clinical pictures resembling mania with flight of ideas.

Euphoria classically occurs in disseminated sclerosis, where it is usually associated with a sense of well-being or eutonia. This is not always so, as some patients with this disease are depressed and despondent. Euphoria and a general passive attitude are characteristic features of the amnestic syndrome. Silly euphoria with lack of foresight and general indifference is found in frontal lobe lesions, particularly when the orbital surface of the frontal lobe is damaged. This silly foresightless indifference is known as *moria* or *Witzelsucht*.

Ecstasy is an exalted state of feeling and is therefore different from the morbidly cheerful mood or elation. The ecstatic state is a sense of extreme well-being associated with a feeling of rapture, bliss and grace. Unlike elation, it is not associated with overactivity and flight of ideas. The mind is usually occupied with a feeling of communion with God, the Saints, or the Infinite. Visions of religious themes and voices of Higher Beings may be seen and heard. Ecstasy may occur in happiness psychosis, schizophrenia and epilepsy.

5. Morbid disorders of emotional expression

Inadequacy and incongruity of affect are characteristic of schizophrenia. In some schizophrenics there seems to be a complete loss of all emotional life so that the patient is indifferent to his own well-being and that of others. In its mildest forms, it shows itself as a (recently acquired) insensitivity to the subtleties of social intercourse. This is known as inadequacy or blunting of affect and was called 'parathymia' by Bleuler. In other cases there seems to be a loss of the direction of emotions, so that an indifferent event may produce a severe affective outburst, but an event which appears emotionally charged to the examiner has no effect on the patient's emotional expression. Some authors have pointed out that incongruity of affect is not necessarily a primary disorder of affect. Bumke, for example, argued that formal thought disorder would lead to a distortion of the schizophrenic's comprehension of his environment, so that although the affect expressed might appear incongruous to the outsider, it might be congruous with the patient's thoughts. Some schizophrenics have a stiffening of affect in that their emotional expression is congruous at first but it does not change as the situation changes.

In chronic hebephrenia the abnormality of emotional expression may occur against the background of an enduring mood state, such as silly euphoria, careless indifference, querulous ill-humour, and autistic depression. Some chronic paranoid schizophrenics produce their delusions and discuss their hallucinations without much emotion, so that there is a clear blunting of affect. Others, however, produce grandiose and expansive delusions with great enthusiasm and persecutory delusions with marked bitterness. These patients are usually elated or depressed and irritable respectively, but outside their delusions they show some emotional blunting.

Before one can diagnose schizophrenia in the presence of affective blunting or incongruity these signs must be unequivocally present. Dissociation of affect, the affectionless personality, and the effects of anxiety may lead to difficulties in diagnosis. The first has already been dealt with. The affectionless psychopath has in general no affection for anyone, so that his cold, emotionally callous attitude may lead to the mistaken diagnosis of schizophrenia. It is in fact rare for someone to have no feeling for any other creature, so that one often finds that the affectionless personality is devoted to a cat, dog, or other animal, or even to one human being. Some depressives, particularly those in middle age, are able to smile and make wry jokes about their condition with a kind of 'gallow's humour'. Similarly, some anxious patients, particularly women, may laugh or smile when talking about painful or embarrassing topics. Neither of these should be mistaken for incongruity of affect.

Something should be said here about the so-called 'smiling depression'. Smiling is normally an expression of cheerfulness, contentment or well being, but it has an important function in communication between persons. There are also the smiles that indicate friendliness, that ask for help and there is the placatory smile. Doubtless an artist can distinguish between them, but undoubtedly psychiatrists cannot. They should, however, be able to distinguish between these smiles and the smiles of cheerfulness. Depressives are anything but cheerful, but unless they are overwhelmed by their miseries or suffering from psychomotor retardation, they can produce the communicatory smile. Psychiatrists should not be deceived by it into underestimating the degree of depression. This is particularly important when it comes to assessing the risk of suicide. The experienced observer will notice that these patients smile with their lips but not with their eyes, so that despite their apparent cheerfulness there is a hardness and lack of movement of the muscles around the eyes. Whenever a patient has morbid ideas of a depressive kind and appears to be fairly cheerful, the examiner should probe carefully into the most sensitive areas of the patient's life and watch for the appearance of depression. These patients are particularly sensitive about ideas of guilt and are often extremely disturbed by commiseration, so that they may become obviously depressed or even burst into tears when the examiner sympathizes with them.

Lability of affect in which rapid changes of emotion occur is not strictly a disorder of emotional expression, but is best considered here in relation to so-called 'compulsive' or 'forced' affects. Lability of affect is found in abnormal personalities, such as the appreciation-needing and irresolute psychopaths of Schneider. Some normal subjects are very soft hearted and are easily moved to tears. Affective lability may be morbid when it occurs in organic states, in which it is quite common. It is, for example, characteristic of 'organic neurasthenia'. Patients with morbid depressions may have difficulty in controlling their emotions, so that any distressing event which normally would produce a transient feeling of unhappiness may bring tears to their eyes. Usually these depressives are made worse by sympathy, which may make them weep. Reactive depressives, on the other hand, enjoy sympathy and tend to produce all their resentments when the examiner is sympathetic. Lability of affect is also found in manic patients who show short bursts of depression and weeping.

In affective lability the patient has difficulty in controlling his emotions, but in affective incontinence there is complete loss of control. The expression of emotion in the absence of any adequate cause has been called 'compulsive' affect. This is, however, a misuse of the word 'compulsive' and the terms 'forced weeping' and 'forced laughing' are preferable. Affective incontinence occurs in organic states, particularly in cerebral arteriosclerosis, but is sometimes the result of disseminated sclerosis. In mild cases the patient bursts into tears when a very slightly emotionally charged topic is mentioned, while when the symptom is marked he bursts into tears when spoken to and has no feeling of sadness. Occasionally attacks of forced laughing occur in coarse brain disease, most commonly in disseminated sclerosis.

Chapter 7

Disorders of the Experience of the Self

WHILE the older psychologists were very interested in the experience of the self and self-awareness, most modern English-speaking psychologists avoid any mention of these subjects. This is very easy to do if one is interested in the psychology of the rat, but it is impossible for the psychiatrist to avoid these problems, as many patients complain of changes in self-awareness. In the German literature there have been long discussions on *Ichbewusstsein* or ego consciousness, but as Weitbrecht has pointed out the term 'ego consciousness' is a bad one, because it can be confused with consciousness. He suggests that the term 'self-experience' avoids all misunderstandings. Jaspers has pointed out that there are four aspects of self-experience:

1. The awareness of existence and activity of the self.
2. The awareness of being a unity at any given point of time.
3. The awareness of continuity of identity over a period of time.
4. The awareness of being separate from the environment or, in other words, awareness of ego boundaries.

It is possible to discuss disorders of self-awareness under these four headings, but quite a number of symptoms can be regarded as disturbance in two of these four aspects.

1. Disturbance of awareness of self-activity

All events which can be brought into consciousness are associated with a sense of personal possession although this is not usually in the forefront of consciousness. This 'I' quality has been called 'personalization' by Jaspers and may be disturbed in psychological disorders. There are two aspects to the sense of self-activity: the sense of existence and the awareness of the performance of one's actions.

a. *Depersonalization*

A change in the awareness of one's activity occurs when the patient feels that he is no longer his normal natural self and is known as 'depersonalization'. Often this is associated with a feeling of unreality so that the environment is experienced as flat, dull and unreal.

This aspect of the symptom is known as 'derealization'. The feeling of unreality is the core of this symptom, and it is always, to a greater or lesser extent, an unpleasant experience. In this it is completely different from ecstatic states. When patients first experience this symptom they find it very frightening and often think that it is a sign that they are going mad. In the course of time they become accustomed to it. Many patients who complain of depersonalization also state that their capacity for feeling is diminished or absent. This is a subjective experience because to the outside observer there is no loss of ability to respond emotionally and appropriately to any given situation. It is important to remember that depersonalization is not a delusion and it should be distinguished from nihilistic delusions in which the patient denies that he exists or that he is alive, or that the world or other people exist.

An emotional crisis or a threat to life may lead to complete dissociation of affect which can be regarded as an adaptive mechanism which allows the subject to function reasonably without being overwhelmed by emotion. Milder degrees of dissociative depersonalization occur in moderately stressful situations, so that depersonalization is quite a common experience. Thus Dixon found that nearly one-half of a series of college students to whom he administered a questionnaire designed to pick out depersonalization experiences reported this symptom. Although, clinically, depersonalization is more common in females than in males, Dixon found no difference between the incidence of depersonalization experiences in male and female students. However, high anxiety scores correlated with depersonalization experiences in women but not in men. Since dissociative depersonalization is a common experience, it is understandable that many patients will complain of depersonalization when they realize that it is a symptom in which doctors are interested. This explains the increase in complaints of depersonalization among patients in a neurosis unit which follows the admission of a patient with hysterical depersonalization.

Very occasionally the outstanding symptom in depressive states is depersonalization. This may give rise to a mistaken diagnosis of schizophrenia, because the unsophisticated and dull patient may have great difficulty in describing depersonalization and the examiner is misled by the bizarre description of the symptom.

It seems likely that there are three different types of depersonalization which qualitatively are different. This is not in keeping with the work of Sedman and his associates who have investigated the occurrence of depersonalization in schizophrenics, depressives, and organic states. They found that depersonalization was more common in schizophrenia, depression, and organic states when there was a depressive mood and a premorbid insecure personality. In epilepsy depersonalization was more common in patients with psychomotor epilepsy or multiple types of attack, who had depressive states during the epileptic attacks or depressions apart from the attacks. From these findings it would appear that patients with organic states, neuroses, and functional psychoses are more likely to complain of depersonalization if they are normally given to excessive self-observation and suffer from depression. Although depersonalization is more common in depressive states than in other disorders, nevertheless depressed mood does not appear to account for the depersonalization found in schizophrenics and organic states.

b. Loss of emotional resonance

In depression there is not only a general lowering of the mood, but there is a loss of the normal emotional resonance. Normally everyone experiences a series of positive and negative feelings as he encounters both animate and inanimate objects in his environment. In depression this natural emotional resonance may be absent and the patient has the feeling that he cannot feel. This lack of natural feeling is usually most marked when the depressive encounters his loved ones. If he has ideas of guilt, this apparent loss of feeling for his wife and children will make him feel even more guilty and morally reprehensible.

2. Disturbances of the immediate awareness of self-unity

In psychogenic and depressive depersonalization the patient may feel that he is talking and acting in an automatic way. This may lead him to say that he feels as if he is two persons. Naïve or appreciation-needing personalities may leave out the 'as if' and say that they are two people. The subject with demoniac possession may feel that he is two people, himself and the Devil. Some schizophrenics also feel that they are two or more people, although this is not common.

3. Disturbance of the continuity of self

In schizophrenia, patients with mild defect states may feel that they are not the person that they were before the illness. This may be expressed as a sense of change, but fantastic paraphrenics may claim that they died under their old name and have come to life as a new person. This sense of complete change of the personality occurs in religious conversion and is of course referred to by Evangelical Christians as 'being born again'.

Multiple personalities occur in appreciation-needing personalities and are usually the result of the interaction of an extremely naïve psychiatrist and a very suggestible patient. Some intelligent schizophrenics after an acute shift of the illness describe how they seemed to pass from being one personality to being another. Other schizophrenics describe how they seemed to be personifying natural events, animals, and historical figures during the acute illness.

4. Disturbance of the boundaries of the self

One of the most fundamental of experiences is the difference between one's body and the rest of the world. Psychoanalysts believe, apparently on the basis of a casual remark of Freud, that this distinction is acquired in later life and that the young infant is unable to differentiate between itself and the rest of the world, and this despite the fact that no very young infant has ever been known to demand food because another is hungry or to seek comfort because another is in pain. The distinction between what pertains to one's body and what does not rests firmly on the fact that a large and specialized part of the afferent nervous system has the sole purpose for obtaining information about the body, the part known as the proprioceptive system. Knowledge of what is the body and what is not is based on the link between information from the extero- and the proprio-ceptors, a link which is probably learned but which has to be maintained constantly. This can be demonstrated very easily. Anybody who has had a finger anaesthetized knows that when touched it feels like a foreign object, i.e. not part of the body. The same phenomenon occurs when the local anaesthetic for a dental operation produces anaesthesia of the lip. Equally relevant to this is the experience of patients who have lesions of the brain which give rise to disturbances of body image. The physiological schema of the body and the continuity and integrity of memory and psychological function is the basis for the awareness of the 'self'.

Disturbances of body image occur chiefly in organic conditions and also in hypnagogic states and in the schizophrenias. On the rare occasions in which depressives declare that their face has become ugly, it would appear that the statement is to be interpreted in a metaphorical sense.

Most schizophrenic symptoms are aspects of a breakdown of the boundary between self and the environment. In the early stages of acute schizophrenia, the patient may experience this breakdown of the limits of his self as a change in his awareness of his own activity which is becoming alienated from him. This is probably not the same as that which occurs in some depersonalized patients who say that they feel like machines, as if their actions were carried out automatically. Loss of control also occurs in obsessions and compulsions, where the thought or impulse to action is experienced as belonging to the patient but occurring against his wishes. In the alienation of personal action which occurs in schizo-phrenics, the patient has the experience that his actions are under the control of some external power. Alienation of thought has already been discussed in the section on disorders of thinking, but the alienation may affect motor actions (see p. 86) and feelings, in which case it is customary to use the term 'passivity feelings'. The patient knows that his actions are not his own and may attribute this control to hypnosis, radio waves, and so on. One patient expressed his passivity feelings by saying, 'I am a guided missile.' This patient experienced penile erections during the night which he knew were produced by the night nurse influencing him with her thoughts as she sat at her desk some twenty feet away. Some psychiatrists have called these passivity experiences 'made' or 'fabricated' experiences because the patient experiences these phenomena as being made by an outside influence. This term 'made experiences' is also used for apophan-ous experiences when the patient knows that all the events around him are being made for his benefit. Schneider believes that these experiences are first-rank symptoms of schizophrenia, so that if organic disease can be excluded these symptoms are diagnostic of schizophrenia.

Another aspect of loss of the boundary with the environment is seen when the patient knows that his actions and thoughts have an excessive effect on the world around him, and he experiences activity which is not directly related to him as having a definite effect on him. Thus Conrad had a patient during World War II who knew that as he passed urine he made bombs fall on London, while Kahlbaum had a patient who saw a carpet being beaten and asked, 'Why are you beating me?' Thought broadcasting, which we have previously discussed as a variety of thought alienation, can obviously be regarded as the result of the breakdown of ego boundaries, because the patient knows that as he thinks the whole world is thinking in unison.

Chapter 8

Disorders of Consciousness

CONSCIOUSNESS can be defined as a state of awareness of the self and the environment. In the normal fully awake subject the intensity of consciousness varies considerably. If someone is carrying out a difficult experiment his level of consciousness will be at its height, but when he is sitting in an armchair glancing through the newspaper the intensity of his consciousness will be much less. In subjects monitoring a monotonously repetitive set of signals short periods of sleep may occur between signals and are not recognized by the subject, but are shown clearly by changes in the electro-encephalogram.

Before we can discuss the disorders of consciousness we must deal with the problem of attention. This can be active when the subject focuses his attention on some internal or external event, or passive when the same events attract the subject's attention without any conscious effort on his part. Active and passive attention are reciprocally related to each other, since the more the subject focuses his attention the greater must be the stimulus which will distract him, i.e. bring passive attention into action.

Disturbance of active attention shows itself as distractibility, so that the patient is diverted by almost all new stimuli and habituation to new stimuli takes longer than usual. It can occur in fatigue, anxiety, severe depression, mania, schizophrenia and organic states. In abnormal and morbid anxiety, active attention may be made difficult by anxious pre-occupations, while in some organic states and paranoid schizophrenia, distractibility may be the result of a paranoid set. In other acute schizophrenias, distraction may be regarded as the result of formal thought disorder because the patient is unable to keep the marginal thoughts, which are connected with external objects by displacement, condensation, and symbolism, out of his thinking, so that irrelevant external objects are incorporated into his thinking. Attention is affected by set, but in normals most sets are not rigid and are altered as a result of incoming information. In the amnestic syndrome this is not so, and the patient's thinking and observation are dominated by rigid sets, so that perception and comprehension are affected by this selective attention.

Disorders of consciousness are associated with disorders of perception, attention, attitudes, thinking, registration, and orientation. The patient with disturbance of consciousness usually shows, therefore, a discrepancy between his grasp of the environment and his social situation, personal appearance, and occupation. This lack of comprehension in the absence of other florid symptoms of disordered consciousness may lead to a mistaken diagnosis of dementia. The clinical test for disturbance of consciousness is to ask the patient the date, the day of the week, the time of day, the place, the duration of his stay in that place, and so on. In other words, one tests the patient's orientation and if he is disorientated there is a *prima facie* case that he has an organic state. If this is of recent origin then it is an acute organic state with disturbance of consciousness. The major exception to this rule is the chronic hospitalized schizophrenic who may be indifferent or reject all contact, so that he seems to be disorientated. While disorientation in an acute illness is almost diagnostic of disordered consciousness, the absence of this sign does not rule out an acute organic state with a mild disorder of consciousness. Poor performance on intellectual and memory tasks, inability to estimate the passage of time, and changes in the electro-encephalogram may all suggest an acute organic state.

Orientation is normally described in terms of time, place and person. When consciousness is disturbed it affects these three aspects in that order. Orientation in time requires that an individual should maintain a continuous awareness of what goes on around him and be able to recognize the significance of those events which mark the passage of time. When the customary events which mark the passage of time are missing, it is very easy to become more or less disorientated in time. Everybody who has been away on holiday in a strange place or been in hospital for a few days has experienced this. Orientation for place is retained more easily because the surroundings provide some clues, and orientation for person is lost with greatest difficulty because the persons themselves provide the information which identifies them.

If a patient is disorientated for time and place it is customary to say that he is confused. Unfortunately, this word is used in everyday speech to mean 'muddled', 'bewildered', or 'perplexed' and some English-speaking psychiatrists use the word in this sense. In fact most confused patients are perplexed, but this sign is also seen in severe anxiety and acute schizophrenia in the absence of disorientation.

Consciousness can be changed in three ways: it may be dream-like, depressed or restricted.

1. Dream-like change of consciousness

There is some lowering of the level of consciousness which is the subjective experience of a rise in the threshold for all incoming stimuli. The patient is disorientated for time and place, but not for person. The outstanding feature in this state is the presence of visual hallucinations, usually of small animals and associated with fear or even terror. The patient is unable to distinguish between his mental images and perceptions, so that his mental images acquire the value of perceptions. As would be expected, thinking is disordered as it is in dreams and shows excessive displacement, condensation, and misuse of symbols. Occasionally Lilliputian hallucinations occur and are associated with a feeling of pleasure. Elementary auditory hallucinations are common, but continuous voices are rare and organized auditory hallucinations take the form of odd disconnected words or phrases. Rarely, hallucinatory voices occur in association with a dream-like change in consciousness, and if they do, the change of consciousness and the visual hallucinations often disappear in a few days, leaving behind an organic hallucinosis with little or no change in consciousness.´ Other hallucinations of touch, pain, electric feelings, muscle sense, and vestibular sensations often occur. The patient is fearful and often misinterprets the behaviour of others as threats. Thus a patient with delirium tremens said: 'Don't hit me; please, don't hit me' whenever anyone approached, although he had never been subjected to assault. The patient is usually restless and may carry out the actions of his trade, for example a patient who was a deputy 'overman' in a coal-mine became delirious and continually banged on the wall as if he were inserting a charge in the coal face and shouted instructions to his mates. This is known as 'occupational delirium'. When the underlying physical illness is severe, insomnia is marked. Usually the disturbance of consciousness is worse at night.

So far we have been describing acute delirium in which dream-like change of consciousness is the outstanding feature, but milder degrees of delirium occur. Thus a patient may have a general lowering of consciousness during the day and be incoherent and confused. At night delirium occurs with visual hallucinations and restlessness, but improves in the morning. Apart from a lowering of consciousness, there may also be some restriction as well so that the mind is dominated by a few ideas, attitudes, and hallucinations. This milder type of delirium has been called a 'toxic confusional state', but this is an unsatisfactory term and 'subacute delirious state' is a better designation.

In the milder varieties of delirium the patient may have inconsistent orientation, so that he may be able to give his address and say that he is in hospital, but insists that his home is next door although it is several miles away. Orientation may also vary during the twenty-four hours, so that when seen in the morning at about 10 a.m. the patient may be reasonably well orientated, but at night he is utterly confused.

The subacute delirious state may pass over into an amnestic state, into torpor, severe delirium, or a twilight state.

2. Lowering of consciousness

The patient is psychologically benumbed and there is a general lowering of consciousness without hallucinations, illusions, delusions, and restlessness. The patient is apathetic, generally slowed down, unable to express himself clearly, and may perseverate. There is no accepted term for this state which is best designated as 'torpor'. This type of consciousness was very often the result of severe infections, such as typhoid and typhus. It is not uncommonly seen in arteriosclerotic cerebral disease following a cerebrovascular accident. If the history of the illness is not clear the general defect in intelligence, in the absence of hallucinations, may be mistakenly diagnosed as severe dementia, but after some weeks there is a remarkable partial recovery and the patient is left with a mild organic defect.

3. Restriction of consciousness

Here awareness is narrowed down to a few ideas and attitudes which dominate the patient's mind. There is some lowering of the level of consciousness, so that in some cases the patient may only appear slightly bemused and uninformed bystanders may not realize that he is confused. Disorientation for time and place occurs. Some of these patients are relatively well ordered in their behaviour and may wander, but usually they are not able to fend for themselves, like the patient with an hysterical twilight state.

The term 'twilight state' was introduced by Westphal for conditions in which there was a restriction of the morbidly changed consciousness, a break in the continuity of consciousness, and relatively well-ordered behaviour. If one keeps strictly to these criteria then the commonest twilight state is the result of epilepsy. However, this term has been used for any condition in which there is a real or apparent restriction of consciousness, so that simple, hallucinatory, perplexed, excited, expansive, psychomotor, and orientated twilight states have been described.

In severe anxiety the patient may be so preoccupied by his conflicts that he is not fully aware of his environment and finds that he has only a hazy idea of what has happened in the past hour or so. This may suggest to the patient that amnesia is a solution of his problems, so that he 'forgets' his personal identity and the whole of his past as a temporary solution of his difficulties. This restriction of consciousness resulting from unconscious motives is known as an 'hysterical twilight state'. It may be difficult to decide how much the motivation of an hysterical twilight state is unconscious because in some cases the subject seems to be deliberately running away from his troubles. Wandering states with some loss of memory are also called 'fugues', but not all fugues are hysterical, because some depressives start out to kill themselves and wander about indecisively for some days before finding their way home or being stopped by the police. Hysterical fugues are more common in subjects who have previously had a head injury with concussion. It is said that this is probably because they have the pattern of amnesia from their past experience of concussion and can therefore present it as an hysterical symptom.

Chapter 9

Motor Disorders

MOTOR disorders can be regarded as neurological signs and discussed and classified like organic signs. This was the way in which Kahlbaum approached catatonia and this attitude was continued by Wernicke and his most outstanding pupil, Kleist. The other approach to these disorders is to explain them as a result of the patient's conscious or unconscious attitudes, for example a stereotypy is explained on the basis of its symbolic significance. As this book is concerned more with the form of psychiatric signs and symptoms rather than the content, the description of psychiatric motor disorders will not include the various psychodynamic interpretations, which the interested reader can find adequately expounded in other textbooks.

Motor disorders in psychiatric illnesses may be subjective or objective. Subjective motor disorders are one aspect of alienation of thought and action which has been discussed in previous chapters. However, for the sake of completeness the abnormal subjective experiences of motor behaviour will also be discussed here.

I. THE ALIENATION OF MOTOR ACTS

Normally we experience our actions as being our own and as being under our control, although this sense of personal control is never in the forefront of consciousness except when we make a desperate effort to overcome the effects of fatigue or toxic substances which are clouding our consciousness and making it difficult for us to control our bodies. In obsessions and compulsions the sense of possession of the thought or act is not impaired, but the patient experiences the obsession as appearing against his will, so that although he has lost control over a voluntary act he still retains the sense of personal possession of the act. In schizophrenia the patient may not only lose the control over his thoughts, actions, or feelings, but also experiences them as being foreign or manufactured against his will by some foreign influence. Schneider has claimed that when a patient without coarse brain disease experiences his thoughts, actions, or feelings as being foreign this is a symptom of the first rank and diagnostic of schizophrenia. These symptoms are known as ideas or delusions of passivity. The patient may merely assert that his behaviour is controlled from without and be unable to give any further explanation. This is best designated as an experience of passivity. He may, however, develop secondary delusions, which explain this foreign control as the result of radio waves, X-rays, television, witchcraft, hypnosis and so on. This can be called 'a delusion of passivity'.

Some anxious and bewildered patients cannot think clearly and are unable to carry out ordinary volitional activity. They may therefore feel 'as if' they are being controlled by foreign influences. As they have difficulty in thinking and putting their thoughts into words they may give the impression that they know that their thoughts are under foreign control. As this symptom is a first-rank symptom the psychiatrist is likely to ask the anxious and the inhibited confused patient if he has this experience. These patients are likely to take up this suggestion and agree with it because it explains their difficulties in thinking and acting. Experiences of passivity which have been extracted from an anxious perplexed patient by means of leading questions are not diagnostic of schizophrenia, unless the term is used as a diagnostic ragbag.

II. THE CLASSIFICATION OF MOTOR DISORDERS

It is very difficult to classify motor disorders, because although clear-cut individual motor signs, such as stereotypies, can be treated as if they were neurological symptoms, it is difficult to classify more complicated patterns of behaviour. The following classification is a useful way of organizing the facts at our disposal:

1. Disorders of Adaptive Movements:
   a. Disorders of Expressive Movements.
   b. Disorders of Reactive Movements.
   c. Disorders of Goal-directed Movements.
2. Non-adaptive Movements:
   a. Spontaneous Movements.
   b. Abnormal Induced Movements.
3. Motor Speech Disturbances in Mental Disorders:
   a. Attitude to Conversation.
   b. The Flow of Speech.
   c. Mannerisms and Stereotypies.
   d. Perseveration.
   e. Echolalia.
4. Disorders of Posture: Distorted Normal Postures; Manneristic Postures; Abnormal Postures; Stereotyped Postures.
5. Abnormal Complex Patterns of Behaviour:
   a. Non-goal-directed Patterns of Behaviour.
   b. Goal-directed Abnormal Patterns of Behaviour.

1. Disorders of adaptive movements

a. Disorders of expressive movements

Expressive movements involve the face, arms, hands, and the upper trunk. The extent of the expressive movements varies with the emotions, but the range of emotional expression is very different in different cultures and may be markedly different in different individuals in the same culture. Thus the expressive movements of a Southern Italian peasant are very different from those of an upper-class Englishman, but they also differ from those of a Northern Italian business man. In Italy, expressive movements of the hands are a natural accompaniment of speech and certain standard verbal expressions are accompanied with gestures, e.g. the vulgar expression, 'Che me ne frega?' ('Why the hell should I care?') is accompanied by a repeated stroking of the undersurface of the jaw with the back of the right hand. In English, on the other hand, the use of the hands in speech is considered to be vulgar or at least the mark of a foreigner, and the well-marked expression of feelings is frowned upon among the upper classes. This tradition of the 'stiff upper lip' among the 'well-bred' English may lead to difficulties in diagnosis. The wide expansive gestures and cheerful mien of a mildly happy Neapolitan would be indicative of mania if seen in an English public-school 'man', who may allow a flicker of a smile on his lips if pleased.

In depression most patients look sad, unhappy, depressed, and possibly anxious. Veraguth pointed out that the main fold in the upper lid is angulated upwards and backwards at the junction of the inner third with the middle third of the fold. Athanassio described the 'omega sign' which is the occurrence of a fold like the Greek letter omega in the forehead above the root of the nose produced by the excessive action of the corrugator muscle. These signs are artificial in a sense because the examiner does not base his assessment of the facies on them, but takes into account the facial expression and its mobility. In many depressives the facial expression and its lack of mobility are diagnostic, but some intelligent obsessional personalities with a high drive may dissimulate and deny that they are very depressed.

Most people weep if they are unhappy enough, but in Britain, where men are not expected to weep, a depressed man who cries during the interview is likely to be a severe depressive. Tears in British women are not so significant. If depression is suspected the patient should always be asked if he is weeping more often than usual or if he is more easily moved to tears than before. Some depressives may say that they are unable to weep and that they have the idea that they might feel much better if they could 'have a good cry'. In retarded depression all bodily movements, including gestures, are diminished or absent. The patient may walk slowly and be bowed down as if carrying a load on his shoulders, and sits with a peculiar stillness. In agitated or anxious depressions the patient is usually restless and apprehensive. There is no direct relation between the severity of the anxiety and the agitation, because some retarded depressives who are almost stuporose are in fact extremely anxious. Some anxious, agitated, depressed housewives find that housework canalizes their anxious agitation and that they feel better when they are working. This may lead them to turn the house upside down, clean all the cupboards out, and so on, as a self-administered occupational therapy. If the agitation is more marked the patient is very restless and unable to finish anything, so that she frequently begins new tasks only to give up in despair. In extreme agitation the patient is a picture of misery and may sit rocking to and fro, wringing the hands, keening and muttering 'Oh! dear' or 'What shall I do?' repetitively. Since the introduction of electroconvulsive therapy and the increase in the psychiatric facilities for early treatment, this picture of extreme agitated depression is not commonly seen in Britain.

In schizophrenia, especially in catatonia, expressive movements are often disordered. The catatonic has a stiff expressionless face and the expressive movements of the body are scanty. Often the eyes appear to be lively, so that the patient appears to be looking at the world through a mask. The flat, full, expressionless face with a greasy appearance, the so-called 'ointment face', occurs in post-encephalitic parkinsonism, while the face in Parkinson's disease is mask-like, but not greasy.

Excessive grimacing and facial contortions which occur in catatonia are disorders of expression, but are best regarded as stereotypies or the result of parakinesia. In catatonia the rounded lips are sometimes thrust forward in a tubular manner so that they resemble an animal's snout. This is known as *Schnauzkrampf* ('snout spasm') and although it is obviously a disorder of expression it is best regarded as a stereotyped posture (*see* p. 99).

In mania, expressive movements are exaggerated. The patient is unnaturally cheerful and uses wide expansive gestures. From time to time transient depression lasting for a few seconds may interrupt the manic overactivity. This is known as 'emotional lability'.

In ecstasy or exaltation the patient has a rapt intense look and is not restless, overactive, and interfering like the manic. When the ecstasy is extreme the patient is incommunicative and is completely absorbed by the intense experience. In milder ecstatic states the patient may preach or lecture in a high-flown way. Ecstasy is found in the happiness psychosis, schizophrenia, epilepsy, and abnormal personalities with the appropriate religious training.

b. Disorders of reactive movements

These movements are immediate automatic adjustments to new stimuli, such as occurs when the subject flinches in response to a threat or turns towards the source of a novel sound. These movements give rise to a general impression of alertness and adaptation to the environment, so that when they are diminished or lost the patient appears to be stiff and un-responsive in a way which is difficult to describe. Many experienced English-speaking psychiatrists notice the loss of reactive movements and use this sign in diagnosis, although they are unable to designate it.

Reactive movements are lost in the inhibited phase of the motility psychosis although voluntary movements are carried out in a graceful way. Reactive movements are usually affected by obstruction (*see below*) in catatonia, so that in addition to the loss of reactive movements the catatonic has obstruction of voluntary movements, which are also carried out in a stiff disjointed manner. Neurological disorders including parkinsonism may lead to a loss of reactive movements. In severe anxiety reactive movements are prompt and excessive.

c. Disorders of goal-directed movements

Normal voluntary movements are carried out smoothly without any sense of effort on the part of the patient. They reflect the personality of the subject and his current mood state. Psychomotor retardation, which occurs in depressive illnesses, is experienced subjectively as a feeling that all actions have become much more difficult to initiate and carry out. In more severe degrees movements become slow and dragging. The mildest degrees can be detected only by careful observation. There is a lack of expression with furrowed eyebrows, the gaze directed downwards (hence the expression 'to look downcast') and the eyes unfocused. The agitated depressive is easily distracted so that he may have difficulty in initiating a voluntary movement and be unable to carry through a complicated pattern of voluntary movements. The execution of individual movements will, or course, be prompt once they have been initiated. The manic carries out individual actions swiftly, but his general pattern of behaviour is not consistent.

In mental illnesses voluntary movements may be performed with difficulty. Psychomotor retardation in depression slows down all psychic and motor acts. In catatonia *Sperrung*, variously translated as 'blocking' or 'obstruction', gives rise to an irregular hindrance to psychic or motor activity. We have already encountered this symptom as thought blocking (*see* p. 37), but here we are considering the effect of blocking on motor acts. Psychomotor retardation has been compared with the uniform slowing down of a vehicle produced by the steady application of a brake, while obstruction has been compared with the effect of putting a rod between the spokes of a moving wheel.

The patient with obstruction may be unable to begin an action at one time and a little later be able to carry it out with no difficulty. Often the patient, when asked to move a part of his body, begins to make a movement and then stops half-way, because the antagonists come into play. At times a voluntary action seems to break through the obstruction and is carried out rather quickly, as if it had to be completed before the obstruction returned. As pointed out above, obstruction may affect habitual and reactive movements, so that the patient does not protect himself when threatened, allows a fly to remain on his face without brushing it off, or does not turn towards the examiner when spoken to.

Obstruction is common in catatonia and is partly responsible for the

stiff ungainly movements which characterize this condition. The muscle
tension associated with obstruction may be normal, increased, or decreased. The effort needed to overcome obstruction is not related to the
muscle tension or the muscles involved, so that it is not dependent on
peripheral factors, but appears to be a difficulty in carrying out the act
itself. Kleist pointed out that a characteristic feature of obstruction was
'the reaction at the last moment'. The examiner, for example, asks the
patient a question several times and there is no reply, but just as he is
turning away the patient answers.

When obstruction is mild, so that spontaneous and reactive movements
are only occasionally completely obstructed, the catatonic patient's motor
activity appears stiff and awkward. With more severe grades of obstruction akinesia occurs and when the symptom is very marked stupor occurs.
Severe psychomotor inhibition in retarded depression may also lead to
stupor. The different forms of stupor are discussed below (*see* p. 102).

Individual variations in the execution of goal-directed movements may
become so pronounced that the movements are odd and stilted, although
still obviously goal-directed. Unusual repeated performances of a goal-
directed motor action or the maintenance of an unusual modification of
an adaptive posture are known as 'mannerisms'. Examples of this sign
are unusual hand movements while shaking hands, when greeting others,
and during writing, as are also peculiarities of dress, of hair style, and
writing. The strange use of words, high-flown expressions, and movements and postures which are out of keeping with the total situation can
also be regarded as mannerisms. Some German authors have used the
term *bizarreries* as a synonym for mannerism, while others, such as
Bostroem, defined *bizarreries* as grotesque distorted movements and postures, in which no aim or goal can be seen. In order to avoid confusion
this sign will be designated 'stereotypy' in this book and will be discussed
in the section on non-adaptive movements. It must, however, be pointed
out that it may be difficult at times to distinguish between mannerisms
and stereotypies.

Mannerisms can be found in relatively normal subjects, abnormal
personalities, schizophrenia, and in neurological disorders. Some of the
older German neuropsychiatrists suggested that all mannerisms might
result from a neurological disorder of varying severity, but there is no
evidence to support this idea. In the non-psychotic, mannerisms are
likely to occur when the subject has the need to be noticed, but has not the
capacity to be intellectually outstanding or original. In art, manneristic
productions are likely to occur when the artist has an intense desire to
create, but has not the artistic ability nor the right material to be really
creative. In other non-psychotic abnormal personalities, mannerisms
may be the result of a lack of control over motor behaviour, which is often
associated with a lack of self-confidence. This accounts for the frequency
of mannerisms in adolescence, when the teenager is anxious, insecure and

immature, and is uncertain how to comport himself. Schizophrenic mannerisms may result from delusional ideas, but are often best regarded as an expression of the catatonic motor disorder which can be interpreted in terms of some type of 'dynamic' psychology, but cannot be explained. Some of the older German psychiatrists believed that mannerisms might be an attenuated form of negativism, but this is not a very satisfactory explanation. In neurological disorders mannerisms are the result of a lack of co-ordination of pyramidal and extra-pyramidal systems, but it would be better not to use the term for these conditions.

From what has been said so far it is obvious that mannerisms are not diagnostic of schizophrenia or any other psychiatric illness or disorder. When they occur their diagnostic significance can only be evaluated if they are regarded as a part of a total clinical picture.

2. Non-adaptive movements

a. Spontaneous movements

Most normal subjects have motor habits which are not goal-directed and which tend to become more frequent during anxiety. Examples of these habits are scratching of the head, stroking, touching, or pulling the nose, stroking, scratching, or touching the face, putting the hand in front of the mouth, clearing the throat, and so on. These actions have obviously been goal-directed at some time, but have since become spontaneous and not directed towards any goal. Animals prevented from carrying out a normal pattern of behaviour which is usually released by a certain compound stimulus may perform another pattern of movement, which is non-adaptive. This is known as 'displacement activity'. The 'normal' motor habits which we are discussing could be regarded as displacement activity as they tend to occur when the subject is frustrated or is uncertain about his choice of behaviour pattern.

Tics are sudden involuntary twitchings of small groups of muscles and are usually reminiscent of expressive movements or defensive reflexes. As a rule the face is affected so that the tic takes the form of blinking or of distortions of the forehead, nose, or mouth, but clearing of the throat and twitching of the shoulders may also be tics. Some psychiatrists regard tics as psychogenically determined motor habits, but others believe that the patient has a constitutional predisposition to tics and this is brought to light by emotional tension. In some cases tics have a clear physical basis, when, for example, they occur after encephalitis or indicate the onset of torsion dystonia or Huntington's chorea.

Static tremor which occurs in the hands, head, and upper trunk when the subject is at rest is another example of a 'normal' spontaneous movement which tends to occur in the very anxious or frightened subject. As not all anxious subjects are markedly tremulous there is probably an inborn predisposition to tremor. Like any other psychogenic symptom tremor may become an hysterical sympton. In World War I soldiers with an acute fright reaction who were tremulous were diagnosed as suffering from 'shell-shock' and were removed from the battle zone. The tremor then continued as an hysterical symptom because it prevented the soldier from being returned to active service. If he was then discharged from the Army with a pension the tremor continued for the rest of his life. Static tremor is sometimes familial and affects the hands, head and upper trunk. It tends to worsen as the patient grows older. Despite a fairly marked static tremor of the hands, these patients are usually able to carry out voluntary movements accurately. Static tremor also occurs in parkinsonism, alcoholism, and thyrotoxicosis. Organic tremors vary in intensity from day to day and are made worse by emotional disturbances, so that when a tremor is inconstant and well marked during a psychological conflict this does not prove that it is basically psychogenic. Intention tremor which occurs as the goal of the voluntary movement is being reached is the result of cerebellar disorders and is commonly seen in disseminated sclerosis.

In spasmodic torticollis there is a spasm of the neck muscles, especially the sternomastoid, which pulls the head towards the same side and twists the face in the opposite direction. At first the spasm lasts for a few minutes, but it gradually increases until the neck is permanently twisted. The patient may prevent the movement of the head by holding his chin with his hand. Some British psychiatrists and neurologists believe that some cases of spasmodic torticollis are hysterical, but most Continental neuropsychiatrists take the view that the condition is basically neurological, although it may be aggravated by psychogenic factors.

In chorea abrupt jerking movements occur which resemble fragments of expressive or reactive movements. In Huntington's chorea the patient may attempt to disguise the choreic movements by turning them into voluntary or habitual ones. For example, the sudden jerking of the arm may be continued into a smoothing down of the hair at the back of the head. If the disease is not too far advanced the unwary examiner may not realize that the patient has chorea and regard him as being a somewhat restless overactive person. Some apparently 'normal' subjects are hyperactive, so that they can never sit still and are always on the move.

In Huntington's chorea the face, upper trunk, and the arms are most affected by the coarse jerky movements. Snorting and sniffing are often also present. In Sydenham's chorea the movements are less jerky and somewhat slower than in Huntington's chorea. The arms and face are affected and respiration is often irregular because it is made difficult by movements of the spine and the abdominal wall. There is usually widespread hypotonia, sometimes hyporeflexia, and not infrequently a prolongation of the muscular contraction evoked during a tendon reflex (Gordon's phenomenon).

In athetosis the spontaneous movements are slow, twisting and writhing, which bring about strange postures of the body, especially of the hands.

Although choreic and athetotic movements are the result of diseases of the nervous system, rather similar movements are sometimes encountered in catatonia. Parakinetic catatonics are in almost constant motion. They grimace frequently and often produce a smile like a clown. The general overactivity and grimacing led some of the older psychiatrists to call this type of behaviour 'clown-like'. The parakinetic catatonic is usually able to answer simple questions and may be capable of simple routine work. The apparently silly smile and the lack of rigidity may lead the examiner to overlook the parakinesia and regard the patient as hebephrenic. Some catatonics continually interwine their fingers or knead and fiddle with the cloth of their trousers or skirts. These patients also tend to touch and handle everything within reach. It is difficult to decide whether this sign is a variety of localized parakinesia or a stereotypy.

As pointed out above, a stereotyped movement is a repetitive non-goal directed action which is carried out in a uniform way. A stereotypy may be a simple movement or a stereotyped or recurrent utterance. It may be possible to discern the remnants of a goal-directed movement in a stereotypy. In the case of a stereotyped utterance the content may be understandable. Thus a catatonic patient continuously mumbled the words 'Eesa marider', which appeared to be a corruption of 'He is a married man'. Her illness began when she discovered that her fiancé by whom she was pregnant was a married man. Using Freudian concepts or empathic psychology it is often possible to understand a stereotypy, but the understanding of the content of a symptom does not, of course, explain its form.

Verbal stereotypies or recurring utterances are to be found in expressive aphasia (q.v.). Hughlings Jackson had a patient with this variety of aphasia following a severe head injury in a brawl, who thereafter could only say 'I want protection'. This is yet another example of the way in which signs and symptoms in catatonia resemble those in neurological disorders.

b. Abnormal induced movements

Some movements of this kind can be regarded as the result of undue compliance on the part of the patient, while others indicate rejection of the environment. In automatic obedience the patient carries out every instruction regardless of the consequences. Kraepelin used to demonstrate this sign by asking the patient to put out the tongue and then he would prick it with a pin. Patients with automatic obedience or command automatism continued to put out their tongues when asked to, although every time that they did so their tongue was pricked. Although some psychiatrists have used the term 'command automatism' as a synonym for automatic obedience, others such as Bumke have used this term for a syndrome characterized by automatic obedience, waxy flexibility, echolalia, and echopraxia. Automatic obedience most commonly occurs in catatonia, although it is occasionally seen in dementing conditions.

Echopractic patients imitate simple actions which they see, such as hand clapping, snapping the fingers, and so on. Apart from imitating the movements of the examiner, these patients may copy the actions of other patients. In echolalia the patient echoes a part or the whole of what has been said to him. Words are echoed irrespectively of whether the patients understand them or not, so that the echolalic patient will repeat words and phrases in foreign languages which he does not know. It has been suggested that echo speech in children is a conditional reflex which is suppressed when voluntary speech takes over. Echolalia could therefore be the result of disinhibition of a childhood speech pattern. Some non-psychotics may echo the last words which have been said to them. This is particularly likely to occur in nervous embarrassed women. The most exhaustive study in the English literature of the psychological and neurological aspects of echo reactions was written by Stengel in 1947. This author pointed out that echo reactions occurred in the following conditions:

1. Transcortical aphasias and dementing conditions in which similar speech disorders occur.
2. Severe mental subnormality with incomplete development of speech.
3. Epileptic personality deterioration.
4. Clouded consciousness.
5. Catatonia.
6. In the early stages of speech in childhood.
7. Fatigue and inattentiveness in normal subjects.

Transcortical aphasia, which has not been previously discussed in this book, was supposed by Lichtheim to be the result of the interruption of the transcortical connexions of the sensory and motor speech areas. The patient either has difficulty in speaking spontaneously or in understanding speech, but is able to repeat what is said to him and to copy to dictation. If the expressive disorder is most marked it is known as 'transcortical motor aphasia', while if the receptive difficulties are more prominent it is called 'transcortical sensory aphasia'. In the motor variety the lesion is in the third left frontal convolution and in the sensory in the first temporal convolution. Like Stengel, many neurologists hold that echolalia occurs in transcortical aphasias, but Brain claims that organic echolalia is different from the speech repetition of transcortical aphasia and believes that it results from a lesion of the left temporal lobe and the adjacent regions of the parietal lobe.

Stengel suggests that the common factors in conditions in which echo reactions occur are an impulse to speak, a tendency to repetition, and a disorder of the comprehension and expression of speech. Chapman and McGhie have suggested that disorders of perception in schizophrenia may account for echopraxia in that illness. In addition to this Lawson, Chapman and McGhie have shown that schizophrenics have difficulty in understanding speech. Chapman and McGhie interviewed schizophrenics who had suffered from the illness for less than two years and found that some of these patients reported that they had echopraxia from time to time. Careful observation of these patients revealed episodes of echopraxia. These patients reported that echopraxia usually happened when they were trying to communicate with another person. Echopraxia was more common when the patient found it difficult to communicate verbally. Although echopraxia usually took place when the patients were looking at someone else, two patients reported that they echoed the behaviour of a memory image of another person. In some patients echopraxia appeared to be completely automatic, while one patient seemed to be more or less consciously playing different roles and decided which person he should imitate. Chapman and McGhie suggested that echopraxia to memory images lay half-way between 'automatic' and 'voluntary' echopraxia. They also put forward the view that these three different types of echopraxia correspond to the three different stages of imitation in childhood which Piaget has described.

Whilst stereotypy is a spontaneous abnormal movement, perseveration is an induced movement, because it is a senseless repetition of a goal-directed action which has already served its purpose. Thus when a patient is asked to put his tongue out he puts it out and then puts it in when told to, but continues to put it out and in thereafter. Perseveration is even more obvious when speech is affected because the patient is unable to get beyond a word or phrase which he goes on repeating and may repeat in reply to another question. Logoclonia and palilalia are special forms of perseveration. In the latter the patient repeats the perseverated word with increasing frequency, while in logoclonia the last syllable of the last word is repeated, e.g. the patient might say: 'I am well today–ay–ay–ay–ay.' Palilalia and logoclonia occur in coarse brain disease, in particular in Alzheimer's disease. Perseveration is found in catatonia and coarse brain disease.

Freeman and Gathercole investigated perseveration in a group of chronic schizophrenics and in a group of arteriosclerotic and senile dements. They describe three types of perseveration. In the first type, 'compulsive repetition', the act is repeated until the patient receives another instruction. The second type is 'impairment of switching' and here the repetition continues after the patient has been given a new task. In the third type, 'ideational perseveration', the patient repeats words and phrases during his reply to a question. All three types of perseveration were found in chronic schizophrenics and dements, but compulsive repetition was more frequent in schizophrenics and impairment of switching more common among dements, but ideational perseveration was equally common in both groups.

Forced grasping is very common in chronic catatonia, but it is also seen in dementias. The doctor offers his hand to the patient and naturally the patient shakes it, except, of course, in cases of negativism. Then the examiner explains to the patient that on all future occasions when the doctor offers his hand he (the patient) should not touch it. It is very important that the patient is fully aware of the fact that he should not accept the proffered hand. After this the examiner talks to the patient for a few minutes and then offers the patient his hand. If forced grasping is present the patient shakes the examiner's hand. Despite frequent instructions not to touch the examiner's hand the patient continues to do so. The grasp reflex is somewhat different. Here the patient automatically grasps all objects placed in his hand. Sometimes the reflex has to be produced by drawing an object across the palm of the hand. When unilateral in a fully conscious patient the grasp reflex indicates a frontal lobe lesion on the opposite side, but when it is bilateral or occurs in clouded consciousness it merely indicates a widespread disorder of the cerebral cortex, which may or may not be reversible. Some patients grope after an object which has stimulated the palm of the hand. If the examiner rapidly touches the palm and steadily withdraws his finger the patient's hand may follow the examiner's finger, rather like a piece of iron following a magnet. This sign has therefore been called the 'magnet reaction'. This may occur in catatonia and coarse brain disease.

In co-operation or *Mitmachen*, the body can be put into any position without any resistance on the part of the patient, although he has been instructed to resist all movements. Once the examiner lets go of the body the part which has been moved returns to the resting position. This disorder is found in catatonia and neurological disease affecting the brain. *Mitgehen* can be regarded as a very extreme form of co-operation, because the patient moves his body in the direction of the slightest pressure on the part of the examiner. For example, the doctor puts his forefinger under the patient's arm and presses gently, whereupon the arm moves upwards in the direction of the pressure rather like the movement of an 'Anglepoise' lamp. Once the pressure stops the arm returns to its former position. Light pressure on the occiput of a patient, who is standing, leads to bending of the neck, flexing of the trunk, and if the pressure continues the patient may fall forward. This sign is found in a few catatonics, when it is usually associated with forced grasping, echolalia and echopraxia. The pressure needed to produce *Mitgehen* is extremely slight, while in co-operation, the movements occur in response to a moderate expenditure of effort on the examiner's part. When examining for *Mitgehen* and co-operation, as in the elicitation of all types of abnormal compliance, the patient must be made to understand that he is expected to resist the examiner's efforts to move him. If this is not done, the bewildered patient may believe that he is being subjected to special examination, in which he is supposed to co-operate.

Some catatonic patients oppose all passive movements with the same degree of force as that which is being applied by the examiner. This is

known as *Gegenhalten* or opposition. Often this is not obvious when the
passive movements are carried out very gently, and it may only appear
when the examiner attempts to produce brusque, forceful, passive movements.

Negativism can be regarded as an accentuation of opposition and some
of the older authors used the term 'reactive muscle tension' as a synonym
for opposition. The word 'negativism' is often loosely used for hostility,
motivated refusal, and failure to co-operate. The stubborn refractory
behaviour of the disturbed appreciation-needing personality, although
senseless to the doctor, is in fact goal-directed. Some severely agitated
depressives and anxiety psychotics are apprehensive and shrink from all
interference. It is wrong to describe such patients as negativistic. Negativism is an apparently motiveless resistance to all interference and may or
may not be associated with an outspoken defensive attitude. It is found
in catatonia, the severely mentally subnormal, and in dementias. Negativism may be passive when all interference is resisted and orders are not
carried out, or it may be active or command negativism when the patient
does the exact opposite of what he is asked to do, in a reflex way. Some
negativistic patients appear to be angry and irritated, while others are
blunted and indifferent. Kleist described a negativistic patient who after
recovery described unpleasant sensations in the precordium. This led
Kleist to suggest that the emotional state in negativism was closely allied
to anxiety or fright. This is an interesting observation since the negativistic behaviour in negativistic catatonics is almost completely abolished
by phenothiazines and similar drugs.

Negativism depends to some degree on the environment, so that sometimes there is a special object of the negativistic behaviour. Thus fellow
patients evoke the negativistic reaction much less easily than doctors and
nurses. Gross suggested that there was the affective state of negativism
and true catatonic or psychomotor negativism, which had no connexion
with the personality. It is difficult to see how these views can be confirmed
or denied.

Ambitendency can be regarded as a mild variety of negativism or as
the result of obstruction. Bleuler considered this symptom to be an expression of ambivalence of the will. In ambitendency the patient makes a
series of tentative movements which do not reach the intended goal
when he is expected to carry out a voluntary action. For example, when
the examiner puts his hand out to shake hands, the patient moves his
right hand towards the examiner's, stops, starts moving the hand, stops,
and so on, until the hand finally comes to rest without touching the
examiner's hand. The patient appears to be in conflict about moving his
body and this presence of opposing tendencies to action was regarded as
a form of ambivalence by Bleuler. However, ambitendency is often found
in negativistic patients when they are approached carefully and every
effort is made to win their confidence. It can then be looked upon as the

result of a partial breakdown of the negativistic attitude. If the examiner handles the negativistic patient who has ambitendency somewhat brusquely the ambitendency disappears and the negativism becomes obvious. Patients with marked obstruction may make a series of tentative movements before the obstruction prevents all movement. Usually in such a case the body remains for a short period in the position reached when obstruction became absolute, in other words the obstruction is followed by preservation of posture. This does not occur in ambitendency due to negativism.

3. Motor speech disorders in the psychoses

Most of the motor disorders of speech which are found in the psychoses have been mentioned as special examples of other motor signs. At the risk of some repetition the psychotic motor speech disorders will be summarized here.

a. Attitude to conversation

Negativistic patients turn away from all attempts to speak to them, while other schizophrenic patients are unable to maintain a conversation because they are easily distracted. Other schizophrenics appear to have continuous voices which makes it impossible for them to attend to what is being said. Some catatonics and paraphrenics whisper continuously and appear to be speaking to voices. Other catatonics turn towards the examiner when he speaks to them and stare at him with an expressionless face, without saying a word. Another group of catatonics turn towards the speaker with a blank face and reply to every question, whether sensible or not. These patients talk past the point. Patients with confusion psychosis look at the examiner in a puzzled, bewildered way and are mute or have poverty of speech.

b. The flow of speech

Muteness has already been discussed (*see* p. 52). Some patients have a pressure of speech. This is usually associated with flight of ideas in mania, but it also is seen in schizophrenia. Thus fantastic paraphrenics become extremely voluble when describing their fantastic experiences and their speech becomes very muddled. Many schizophasics never stop talking when spoken to and often harangue or lecture the examiner rather than hold a conversation with him.

The quality of speech in catatonia, as in motor aphasia, may be strange and stilted, so that the patient sounds like a foreigner. Other catatonics have an odd intonation, talk in falsetto tone, or have staccato or nasal speech. A few schizophrenic patients never speak above a whisper or speak with a strange strangled voice (*Wurgstimme*). This may be a mannerism or the result of delusions.

c. Mannerisms and stereotypies

The disorders of stress, inflection, and rhythm mentioned in the previous section are mannerisms, but mannerisms of pronunciation also occur. Only a few words may be mispronounced or there may be a distortion of most words, resembling paraphasia. Verbal stereotypies are words or phrases which are repeated. They may be produced spontaneously or be set off by a question. In verbigeration one or several sentences or strings of fragmented words are repeated continuously. For example one of Kraepelin's patients repeated for three hours the following sentences: 'Dear Emily, give me a kiss; we want to get well, a greeting and it would be nothing. We want to be brave and beautiful, follow, follow mother, so that we come home soon. The letter was for me; take care, that I get it.'

Sometimes in verbigeration the patient produces strings of incomprehensible jargon in which stereotypies are embedded. Usually the tone of voice is monotonous. Verbigeration is not always spontaneous but may be produced in answer to questions. It is quite different from schizophasia (speech confusion) in which there is gross thought disorder, but the patient speaks in a normal way with change of intonation and so on.

d. Perseveration

Verbal perseveration can belong to any of the three types of Freeman and Gathercole (*q.v.*). In some cases there is perseveration of theme rather than the actual words and this can be regarded as impairment of switching. In other cases the set or attitude is perseverated and the patient cannot solve a new problem because he cannot break free from his previous set. Verbal perseveration can occur in schizophrenia and organic states.

Some psychologists use the word 'perseveration' in the sense of the ability of the subject to persevere in a task and describe a personality trait of 'perseveration'. This is, of course, not perseveration in the sense that it has been used in this book, but is probably a malapropism for 'perseverance'.

e. Echolalia

As has been pointed out earlier, Stengel has suggested that echo reactions tend to occur in subjects who wish to communicate, but have permanent or transient receptive and expressive speech disorders. Kleist pointed out that some catatonic patients reply to questions by echoing the content of the question in different words. He called this 'echologia'.

4. Disorders of posture

Abnormal postures occur in abnormal personalities who are seeking attention and appreciation. Such individuals are, of course, *poseurs.* Strange postures may also result from nervous habits in disturbed adolescents and over-anxious personalities. Manneristic posture is an odd stilted one which is an exaggeration of a normal posture and not rigidly preserved, while a stereotyped one is an abnormal and non-adaptive posture which is rigidly maintained. It is obvious that the exact point at which a postural mannerism becomes a stereotypy may be difficult to decide. Manneristic postures occur in some schizophrenics when they may be related to delusional attitudes or may be without any understandable basis and therefore catatonic. Although it may be difficult to decide whether some postures are technically manneristic or stereotyped, many stereotyped postures are obvious; as, for example, when a catatonic patient sits with his head and body twisted at right-angles to a vertical plane passing through both hip joints. Other catatonics lie with their heads a few inches off the pillow, a so-called psychological pillow, and maintain this posture for hours. This is a stereotyped posture, which is also found in some dements.

In perseveration of posture the patient tends to maintain for long periods postures which have arisen fortuitously or which have been imposed by the examiner. The patient allows the examiner to put his body into strange uncomfortable positions and then maintains such postures for at least one minute and usually much longer. Sometimes there is a feeling of plastic resistance as the examiner moves the body, which resembles the bending of a soft wax rod, and when the passive movement stops the final posture is preserved. Wernicke called this 'waxy flexibility' or *flexibilitas cerea*. In many cases of preservation of posture there is no resistance to passive movements but as the examiner releases the body those muscles which fix the body in the abnormal position can be felt to contract. This is not waxy flexibility and should be called either 'preservation of posture' or 'catalepsy'.

In some patients catalepsy has to be evoked by putting the patient's arm in a comfortable position and if this is maintained, the arm is put into a series of unusual positions each of which is more uncomfortable than the previous one, so that finally the patient will preserve very strange postures. If gentle passive movements fail to elicit catalepsy it can sometimes be evoked by jerking the arm or leg rather brusquely into a strange position.

The patient must always be told at first that he is not obliged to leave his body in the position in which it is put by the examiner. If this is not done the patient may believe that he is supposed to maintain the posture as part of a test. Bleuler suggested that the examiner should lift the patient's arm by the wrist and take the pulse. If when the arm is released it does not return to the resting position then catalepsy is present, as the normal person would naturally realize that he could put his arm down once the doctor has finished feeling his pulse.

Although catalepsy often occurs in mute stuporose catatonics it is also found in mild states of akinesia. On occasions it occurs at the same time as obstruction, so that when the obstruction stops, the patient in the middle of an action catalepsy maintains the body in this mid-flight position for some time. Catalepsy usually lasts for more than one minute and ends with the body slowly sinking back into the resting position. Catalepsy is often very variable and may disappear for a day or so only to return again. Although waxy flexibility and catalepsy occur in catatonia, they are also met with in diseases, such as encephalitis, vascular disorders, and neoplasms, affecting the mid-brain.

5. Abnormal complex patterns of behaviour
a. Non-goal-directed patterns of behaviour

The two important patterns of behaviour of this type are stupor and excitement, which although diametrically opposed patterns of behaviour, often occur in the same psychiatric disorders.

Bumke defined stupor as 'a state of more or less complete loss of activity with no reaction to external stimuli'. It can be regarded as an extreme state of hypokinesia. Psychomotor inhibition and obstruction may produce a general slowing down of activity, and as these disorders become more severe the patient's condition approaches stupor. Completely stuporose patients are mute, but in sub-stuporose states patients may reply briefly to questions in muttered monosyllables. Stupor may occur in fright neuroses, hysteria, depression, cycloid psychoses, catatonia and coarse brain disease.

Psychogenic stupor occurs in severe fright neuroses, such as those which occur during a severe bombardment. The patient is as it were 'paralysed with fear' and is unable to retreat from danger. In less severe cases he may be virtually mute but not completely motionless and may at times wander about slowly in a small area in a very bewildered way. This stupor can be terminated by sedation and reassurance. A moderate dose of an anxiolytic drug sufficient to produce sleep should be given. In hysterical stupor, which is not common, the patient retreats from his problem by becoming mute and motionless. Sometimes an hysterical stupor is the hysterical prolongation of a fright neurosis, so that the disorder begins as an acute psychogenic reaction to severe trauma and then becomes a goal-directed reaction; that is, it is presented by the patient for some gain, although he is not fully aware of this motivation. Incontinence of urine rarely if ever occurs in hysterical stupor and these patients tend to eat when no one is observing them. Reassurance coupled with hypnosis or small doses of intravenous sodium amylobarbitone will usually lead to the uncovering of the conflict and its disappearance. Hysterical stupor is more likely to occur in primitive unsophisticated subjects or in grossly disturbed appreciation-needing personalities.

Space-occupying lesions affecting the third ventricle, the thalamus and the mid-brain produce a stuporose state in which the eyes are open, the patient appears to be alert, reacts slightly to painful stimuli, and is uncooperative. This has been called 'akinetic mutism', which is a bad term since these patients have a general lowering of the level of consciousness, failure to register new memories, and total amnesia for the episode if they recover.

Stupor may occur in epilepsy when there is a continuous epileptic discharge in the electro-encephalogram or repeated bursts of such discharges. A few patients have recurrent catatonic stupor in which the electro-encephalogram shows continuous spike and wave discharges. This has been called 'petit mal status' and regarded as a special variety of status epilepticus. Patients with Gjessing's periodic catatonia have very slow waves in the electro-encephalogram during the reaction phase. In one case 2-cycles-per-second waves were found.

Although stupor occurs in depression and the cycloid psychoses the commonest variety of 'functional' psychosis in which stupor occurs is catatonic schizophrenia. Very occasionally patients in catatonic stupor have pure akinesia and all muscles are flaccid. Usually the muscle tension is permanently increased or it varies from time to time and is associated with obstruction. At times the muscle tension is so marked that the patient is like a block of wood. The muscle tension in catatonic stupor is usually increased in the muscles of the forehead and the masseters. *Schnauzkrampf* (*q.v.*) is sometimes seen. The sternomastoid muscles are usually contracted, giving rise to the psychological pillow. Opposition or reactive muscle tension may also occur. Increased or reactive muscle tension is usually most marked in the anterior neck muscles, the masseters, the muscles around the mouth, and the proximal muscles of the limbs. Tension may be increased permanently or it may disappear and return for varying periods of time. Very rarely all muscles are flaccid with the exception of one group in which tension is markedly increased. The face is usually stiff and devoid of expression, giving rise to 'a dead-pan' expression, but often the eyes are lively and contrast with the lack of facial expression. Usually there is no emotional response to affect-laden questions, so that the patient is not disturbed by painful personal questions. As a rule the response to painful stimuli is absent and the patient does not respond to any threat to his existence. Catalepsy may be present. Incontinence of urine is the rule and faecal incontinence may occur. The stupor can often be interrupted by an intravenous injection of 0·2–0·5 g. of sodium amylobarbitone and this procedure should be carried out in all stupors in which coarse brain disease has been excluded. Some patients, particularly with acute schizophrenia, have vivid hallucinatory experiences and their failure to respond is due to a preoccupation with these symptoms. Thus one virtually mute patient was given 0·3 g. of sodium amylobarbitone and began to speak slowly about his delusional experiences. When asked why he spoke in this way he replied: 'So would you if you had been travelling in a space ship for six days.' This patient had had intense schizophrenic hallucinatory and delusional experiences which had absorbed him so completely that he had become stuporose. In other cases, however, the patient is unable to explain his experiences when stuporose and can only produce odd fragments of what he may describe as a 'bad dream'.

Stupor may occur in inhibited confusion and motility psychoses. In the confusion psychosis the patient is obviously perplexed and bewildered. If he is able to speak he may often admit to delusions of reference and significance. Leonhard claims that bewildered stupor is diagnostic of inhibited confusion psychosis and that the presence of primary delusional experiences in a bewildered patient with a near-stuporose state is not diagnostic of schizophrenia. In motility psychosis the reactive and expressive movements are affected more than the voluntary ones, so that the patient may be motionless and yet be able to carry out voluntary movements on request. Obstruction, opposition, catalepsy and increased muscle tension are not found in inhibited motility psychosis. Although patients with catatonic stupor are motionless to a large degree, quite a number have slight stereotyped movements of the hands or fingers. This does not occur in stupor resulting from the cycloid psychoses. Leonhard believes that this combination of inhibition and excitation is typical of catatonia.

Today depressive stupor is not very common in Britain, although patients with moderate psychomotor retardation are still seen fairly frequently. The patient in depressive stupor looks depressed and becomes more depressed when affect-laden topics, such as his family affairs, are mentioned by the examiner. Sometimes the facial expression is more that of anxiety and bewilderment. Catalepsy, obstruction, stereotypies, changes in muscle tone, and incontinence of urine and faeces do not occur.

The older textbooks discussed the clinical differentiation of depressive from catatonic stupor, but as both are usually rapidly terminated by electroconvulsive treatment this is a somewhat useless exercise. In catatonic stupor the outstanding features are a 'dead-pan' facial expression, changes in muscle tone, catalepsy, stereotypies, and incontinence of urine. These are in contrast with the depressive facies, the normal muscle tone, the response to emotional stimuli, and the absence of incontinence in depressive stupor.

The possibility of a neurological disorder should never be overlooked in a rapidly developing stupor. An electro-encephalogram should be performed wherever possible and if there is the slightest possibility of coarse brain disease a lumbar puncture should be carried out. Once organic disease has been excluded then the stupor may be reversed by an intravenous injection of sodium amylobarbitone.

Although excitement appears to be the opposite of stupor it often occurs in the same mental illnesses. In some cases it can be understood as being secondary to some other psychological abnormality. Thus in paranoid schizophrenia a sudden increase in the intensity of hallucinatory voices may lead to an excitement. In appreciation-needing personalities excitements are motivated by a desire for attention or have the object of imposing a solution of the patient's problems on the environment. In mania the excitement can be understood as a natural consequence of the elated mood. However, some excitements, such as those which occur in catatonia and coarse brain disease, cannot be understood as arising from some other psychological abnormality.

Psychogenic excitements may be acute reactions or goal-directed reactions. Predisposed subjects may react to moderately stressful situations with senseless violence. Kretschmer compared such chaotic behaviour to the 'storm of movement' which occurs in the trapped animal which cannot find its way out of the trap. Thus the bird which has flown into a room through a slightly open window flutters about wildly until it accidentally finds the open window. Chaotic restlessness rather like a 'storm of movement' may occur in susceptible subjects during earthquakes, other catastrophes, heavy bombardment, and so on. It may also occur in unsophisticated and mentally subnormal persons subjected to mild stress. Thus a peasant from an isolated region may become acutely excited after admission to a busy general hospital, which he experiences as a strange threatening environment. In goal-directed psychogenic reactions excitement is a part of attention-seeking behaviour. This reaction occurs in adolescent and young adult women who have been unhappy and disturbed since childhood. They attack others, smash furniture and windows, and repeatedly mutilate themselves. Usually even during severe excitement it is possible to make contact with these patients and interrupt the overactivity. These patients seem eager to be punished and enjoy a good fight. Often they complain of visual hallucinations, particularly of men, but they do not show any clear schizophrenic symptoms.

Excitement occurs in moderately severe agitated depressives, in which it takes a somewhat mechanical form. The patients wander about restlessly and bewail their fate monotonously. In severe agitated depression the patient, usually a woman, wrings her hands continuously, sits up in bed, rocks to and fro, and laments, repeating such phrases as 'Oh dear!' and 'What shall I do?' Sometimes they pick at their fingers or rub their faces. The total picture is one of abject misery.

In typical manic excitement the patient is cheerful, restless, and interfering, with flights of ideas (q.v.). If the excitement becomes intense then the patient rushes about the place and may shout incessantly. These patients may rapidly exhaust themselves and develop intercurrent physical illnesses. Usually the mood in hypomania and mania is cheerful, but sometimes the patient is angry and irritable. Such patients are likely to become violent or threatening when thwarted. Occasionally the mood is one of angry irritation throughout the illness and the patient is querulous and complaining.

In the motility psychosis excitement takes the form of restless overactivity with a clown-like or theatrical quality. The movements are graceful and no stereotypies occur. These patients do not have the very angular stiff movements of catatonia, but if the excitement is very severe repetitive movements such as rocking to and fro may occur. As these patients are overactive and not obviously cheerful they may be diagnosed as suffering from hebephrenia or catatonia.

In catatonic excitements the face is 'dead pan' and the movements of the body are often stiff and stilted. The violence is usually senseless and purposeless.

In delirium there may be ill-directed overactivity, but occasionally occupational delirium occurs (*q.v.*). Many delirious patients are extremely frightened so that they become more excited when approached by doctors and nurses, whom they think are going to attack them. If the physical condition is not too debilitating the delirious patient may try to escape his alleged persecutors and in doing so kill or harm himself. For example, a delirious patient may jump through a window several stories up in an attempt to escape. It is important to remember that the delirious patient can be reassured if one takes the time and the trouble to speak loudly and slowly. Epileptic furore and pathological drunkenness are two special forms of organic excitement. In the first the patient becomes senselessly violent and indiscriminately destructive during an epileptic confusional state. In pathological drunkenness there is an excitement with senseless violence after the patient has drunk a small quantity of alcohol. The episode lasts an hour or so and the patient has a complete amnesia for it. Although it is called drunkenness, the patient is not ataxic and does not have the usual signs of drunkenness. Often the patient is murderously aggressive. For example, one British soldier after drinking a few pints of beer raked a dance hall with his sub-machine gun killing three people, and in another case a man brutally murdered his wife after drinking three bottles of beer and in the morning woke up to find himself covered in blood but with no memory for the events leading up to his wife's death.

It is difficult to classify impulsive actions. Here they will be regarded as non-goal-directed complex patterns of behaviour. Most 'normal' people have at some time acted on impulse or on the spur of the moment. The dynamic psychologists attribute these actions to unconscious motives. Some abnormal personalities are very prone to impulsive actions. Such subjects may suddenly wander away from their work and homes on impulse, or steal in circumstances in which they are certain to be detected. Impulsive actions, usually of an aggressive kind, are common in catatonia. Thus a patient may suddenly strike another, throw a plate, or smash a window. It is impossible to find any rational reason for such actions.

b. Goal-directed abnormal patterns of behaviour

Abnormal patterns of behaviour of this type occur in nearly all psychiatric syndromes, so that only a few such patterns associated with severe psychiatric disorders can be discussed here.

Some schizophrenics, usually silly hebephrenics, behave in a childish spiteful way to other patients and even to doctors and nurses. They may pull chairs away from other patients who are about to sit down, punch other patients when no one is looking, and so on. One patient, who was usually employed scrubbing floors, would wait until a doctor had walked past her and then throw the scrubbing brush at his head with unerring accuracy. Manics also play practical jokes, e.g. one patient would creep behind a nurse who was about to leave the ward to go into the hospital grounds and put pieces of coal in the hood of her cape, so that when she pulled the hood over her head to protect herself from the rain she was covered by a shower of coal. Apart from the silly hebephrenics and manics some abnormal personalities get great pleasure from practical jokes. When their unfortunate victims complain about the stupid, tasteless, unpleasant jokes they are regarded as 'poor sports'. This practical joking is really a special form of aggressive behaviour, for which the practical joker is often not punished, because it satisfies the *Schadenfreude* of the bystanders.

Brutal and aggressive behaviour is often socially determined, because in some communities violence is an accepted method of settling disputes. However, not all aggressive abnormal personalities come from this type of background. On the whole, aggression is not very common in chronic functional disorders. Surprisingly few schizophrenics with persecutory delusions attack their alleged persecutors. Aggressiveness in chronic schizophrenics seems to be more common in those patients who come from backgrounds in which violent behaviour is common. Some schizophrenics with gross blunting of affect may become brutal and unnecessarily aggressive when thwarted or interfered with, although they are well behaved if left alone. As pointed out during the discussion of delusions (*see* p. 48) delusion-like ideas of marital infidelity are more likely to give rise to violent or murderous behaviour than are true delusions of persecution. The jealous husband may beat or even torture his wife in order to extract a confession of infidelity. For example, one jealous husband tied up his wife, who was five months pregnant, inserted match-sticks under her toenails and set light to them, in order to persuade her to confess to adultery.

In the popular mind murder is associated with madness, but in Britain most murderers are unhappy abnormal people who resort to murder as the only way out of their difficulties. Some murderers suffer from organic states, particularly those resulting from epilepsy. Schizophrenics may murder alleged persecutors, carry out instructions to murder given by hallucinatory voices, or kill others as 'sacrifices' in conformance with grandiose religious beliefs. Depressives may murder their loved ones before committing suicide themselves. These patients are usually deluded and believe that they have incurable inherited insanity or some foul disease which they have passed on to their children who are also doomed to suffer. The children are therefore murdered in the mistaken belief that they would be 'better off dead'. This type of murder is known as 'extended suicide'.

Promiscuity is not in itself an indication of mental disorder, although in the past promiscuous female dullards from the lower classes have been detained as mentally subnormal, while their middle-class sisters with the same proclivities went scot-free. Disinhibition resulting from coarse brain disease, mania, or schizophrenia may give rise to promiscuous behaviour. Thus the female manic has a greater risk of becoming pregnant, while the male is more liable to contract venereal disease. Sometimes sexual perversions appear for the first time after the onset of coarse brain disease or schizophrenia. In some schizophrenics the point of onset of the illness cannot be determined and there is a slow, steady, ethical, and moral deterioration which finally becomes so marked that it is obvious that there has been a schizophrenic process at work. The women may become prostitutes in their drift down the social scale, whereas the men are likely to become drifters and petty thieves.

Bibliography

THE signs and symptoms of mental illness were first described in detail by the great French and German clinical psychiatrists of the nineteenth century and many of their descriptions have been repeated almost unchanged to the present day. For example, little has been added to the clinical descriptions of hallucinations and illusions which Kahlbaum wrote in 1866. It was therefore decided to restrict the references to review articles and recent investigations. There are some works which have a bearing on most sections of this book and in order to avoid repetition they will be listed here. The reader requiring further information on any part of this book is advised to consult these works in addition to those cited in connexion with each chapter.

BLEULER, E. (1951), *Dementia Praecox or the Group of Schizophrenias* (trans. ZINKIN, J.). London: Allen & Unwin.

BUMKE, O. (1928), *Handbuch der Geisteskrankheiten* (Handbook of Mental Diseases), vols. 1, 2. Berlin: Springer.

CAMERON, N. (1947), *The Psychology of the Behaviour Disorders*. Boston: Houghton & Mifflin.

— — (1963), *Personality Development and Psychopathology*. Boston: Houghton & Mifflin.

FISH, F. J. (1962), *Schizophrenia*. Bristol: Wright.

— — (1964), *An Outline of Psychiatry*. Bristol: Wright.

JASPERS, K. (1962), *General Psychopathology* (trans. HAMILTON, M. W., and HOENIG, J.). Manchester: Manchester University Press.

KRAEPELIN, E. (1909), *Psychiatrie. Ein Lehrbuch für Studierende und Aerzte* (Psychiatry. A Textbook for Students and Practitioners), vol. 1. Leipzig: Barth.

— — (1919), *Dementia Praecox and Paraphrenia* (trans. BARCLAY, M.). Edinburgh: Livingstone.

— — (1921), *Manic Depressive Insanity and Paranoia* (trans. BARCLAY, M.). Edinburgh: Livingstone.

TAYLOR, F. K. (1966), *Psychopathology. Its Causes and Symptoms*. London: Butterworths.

Chapter 1. Introduction

The general problems of psychiatric disorders are not often discussed in English. The works by Jaspers and Taylor referred to above are the most easily accessible works which deal with this matter adequately. Other publications relevant to this chapter are:

BINSWANGER, L. (1958), 'The existential analysis school of thought', in *Existence. A New Dimension in Psychiatry* (ed. MAY, R., ANGEL, E., and ELLENBERGER, H. F.). New York: Basic Books.

FISH, F. J. (1961), 'Existentialism and psychiatry', *Br. J. Psychiat.*, **107**, 878.

SCHNEIDER, K. (1958), *Psychopathic Personalities* (trans. HAMILTON, M. W.). London: Cassell.

Chapter 2. Classification of Psychiatric Disorders

FISH, F. (1964), 'The cycloid psychoses', *Comp. Psychiat.*, **5**, 155.

— — (1964), 'A guide to the Leonhard classification of chronic schizophrenia', *Psychiat. Q.*, **38**, 438.

LEONHARD, K. (1959), *Die Aufteilung der endogenen Psychosen* (The Classification of the Endogenous Psychoses), 2nd ed. Berlin: Akademie Verlag.

LEONHARD, K., and VON TROSTORFF, S. (1964), *Prognostische Diagnose der endogenen Psychosen* (Prognostic Diagnosis of the Endogenous Psychoses). Jena: Fischer.

PETRILOWITSCH, N. (1966), *Abnorme Persönlichkeiten* (Abnormal Personalities), 3rd ed. Basle: Karger.

SCHNEIDER, K. (1959), *Clinical Psychopathology* (trans. HAMILTON, M. W.). New York: Grune & Stratton.

STENGEL, E. (1960), 'Classification of mental disorders', *Bull. Wld Hlth Org.*, **21**, 601.

Chapter 3.   Disorders of Perception

BARBER, T. X. (1964), 'Towards a theory of "hypnotic" behaviour: Positive visual and auditory hallucinations', *Psychol. Rec.*, **14**, 197.

—— and CALVERLY, D. S. (1964), 'An experimental study of "hypnotic" (auditory and visual) hallucinations', *J. abnorm. soc. Psychol.*, **68**, 13.

BURCHARD, J. M. (1963), 'Ueber die Struktur der optischen Wahrnehmung und ihrer krankhaften Störungen' (The structure of visual perception and its morbid disorders), *Fortschr. Neurol. Psychiat.*, **33**, 277.

—— (1965), *Untersuchungen zur Struktur symptomatischen Psychosen* (Investigations of the Structure of Symptomatic Psychoses). Stuttgart: Enke.

GLONING, I., GLONING, K., and HOFF, H. (1958), 'Die Halluzinationen in der Hirnpathologie' (Hallucinations in brain disorders), *Wien. Z. NervHeilk.*, **14**, 289.

GOULD, L. N. (1950), 'Verbal hallucinations as automatic speech', *Am. J. Psychiat.*, **107**, 110.

HARE, E. H. (1973), 'A short note on pseudo-hallucinations', *Br. J. Psychiat.*, **122**, 469.

HERON, W., BEXTON, W. H., and HEBB, D. O. (1953), 'Cognitive effects of decreased variation in the sensory environment', *Am. Psychol.*, **8**, 366.

HILLERS, F. (1963), 'Ueber Halluzinationen bei Schizophrenen. Teil I' (Hallucinations in schizophrenics. Part I), *Psychiatria Neurol.*, **145**, 100.

—— (1963), 'Ueber Halluzinationen bei Schizophrenen. Teil II' (Hallucinations in schizophrenics. Part II), *Ibid.*, **145**, 129.

HOCH, P. M., and ZUBIN, J. (eds.) (1965), *Psychopathology of Perception*. New York: Grune & Stratton.

INGLIS, J. (1965), 'Sensory deprivation and cognitive disorders', *Br. J. Psychiat.*, **111**, 309.

JASPERS, K. (1911), 'Zur Analyse der Trugwahrnehmungen (Leibhaftigkeit und Realitätsurteil)' (Analysis of sense deceptions—Substantiality and reality judgement), *Z. ges. Neurol. Psychiat., Originalien*, **6**, 460.

—— (1912), 'Die Trugwahrnehmung' (Sense deceptions), *Ibid., Referate*, **4**, 289.

LEFF, J. P. (1968), 'Perceptual phenomena and personality in sensory deprivation', *Br. J. Psychiat.*, **114**, 1499.

LEIBALDT, G., and KLAGES, W. (1961), 'Morphologische Befunde bei einer isolierten chronischen taktilen Dermatazoenhalluzinose' (Pathological findings in an isolated chronic tactile infestation hallucinosis), *Nervenarzt*, **32**, 157.

LEISCHNER, A. (1961), 'Die autoskopischen Halluzinationen—Heautoskopie' (Autoscopic hallucinations—heautoscopy), *Fortschr. Neurol. Psychiat.*, **29**, 550.

LEWIS, A. J. (1932), 'The experience of time in mental disorders', *Proc. R. Soc. Med.*, **25**, 611.

LHAMON, W. T., and GOLSTONE, S. (1956), 'The time sense. Estimation of one second duration by schizophrenic patients', *Archs Neurol. Psychiat., Chicago*, **76**, 625.

—— —— —— and GOLDFARB, J. L. (1965), 'The psychopathology of time judgement', in *Psychopathology of Perception* (ed. HOCH, P. H. and ZUBIN, J.). New York: Grune & Stratton.

LHERMITTE, J. (1951), 'Visual hallucinations of self', *Br. med. J.*, **1**, 431.

LUKIANOWICZ, N. (1958), 'Autoscopic phenomena', *Archs Neurol. Psychiat., Chicago*, **80**, 199.

McCONNELL, W. B. (1965), 'The phantom double in pregnancy', *Br. J. Psychiat.*, **111**, 67.

McKELLAR, P. (1957), *Imagination and Thinking*. London: Cohen & West.

MATUSSEK, P. (1963), 'Wahrnehmung, Halluzinationen und Wahn' (Perception, hallucinations and delusion), in *Psychiatrie der Gegenwart* (ed. GRUHLE, H. W., JUNG, R., MAYER-GROSS, W., and MUELLER, M.), vols. 1, 2. Berlin: Springer.

MAYER-GROSS, W. (1928), 'Psychopathologie und Klinik der Trugwahrnehmung' (Psychopathology and clinical features of sense deceptions), in *Handbuch der Geisteskrankheiten* (Handbook of Mental Diseases), (ed. BUMKE, O.), vol. 1. Berlin: Springer.

MEYER, J. E. (1952), 'Der Bewusstseinszustand bei optischen Sinnestäuschungen' (The state of consciousness in visual sense deceptions), *Archs Psychiat. Nervenkr.*, **189**, 477.

MUELLER, C. (1956), *Mikropsie und Makropsie*. Basle: Karger.

ORME, J. E. (1966), 'Time estimation and the nosology of schizophrenia', *Br. J. Psychiat.*, **112**, 37.

OSWALD, I. (1962), *Sleeping and Waking*. Amsterdam: Elsevier.

PENFIELD, W., and PEROT, P. (1963), 'The brain's record of auditory and visual experience', *Brain*, **86**, 595.

SCHROEDER, P. (1926), 'Das Halluzinieren' (Hallucinating), *Z. ges. Neurol. Psychiat.*, **101**, 599.

SEDMAN, G. (1966), 'A comparative study of pseudo-hallucinations, imagery and true hallucinations', *Br. J. Psychiat.*, **112**, 9.

— — (1966), 'A phenomenological study of pseudo-hallucinations and related experiences', *Acta psychiat. scand.*, **42**, 35.

STEIN, J. (1928), 'Ueber die Veränderung der Sinnesleistungen und die Enstehung von Trugwahrnehmungen' (On the change in sensory performance and the formation of sense deceptions), in *Handbuch der Geisteskrankheiten*, (ed. BUMKE, O.), vol. 1. Berlin: Springer.

TERESA OF AVILA (1957), *The Life of Saint Teresa of Avila by Herself* (trans. COHEN, J. M.). Harmondsworth, Mdx.: Penguin Books.

TODD, J., and DEWHURST, K. (1955), 'The double: Its psychopathology and psychophysiology', *J. nerv. ment. Dis.*, **122**, 47.

TYEREL, G. N. M. (1953), *Apparitions*, 2nd ed. London: Duckworth.

VERBEEK, E. (1959), 'Le Délire dermatozairre et le Problème de l'Hallucinose tactile chronique' (The delusion of infestation and the problem of chronic tactile hallucinosis), *Psychiatria Neurol.*, **138**, 217.

WEISMAN, A. D., and HACKETT, T. P. (1958), 'Psychosis after eye surgery', *New Engl. J. Med.*, **258**, 1284.

Chapter 4. Disorders of Thought and Speech

ARTHUR, A. Z. (1964), 'Theories and explanations of delusions. A review', *Am. J. Psychiat.*, **131**, 105.

ASHER, R. (1951), 'Munchausen syndrome', *Lancet*, **1**, 339.

ASTRUP, C. (1962), *Schizophrenia–Conditional Reflex Studies*. Springfield, Ill.: Thomas.

BANNISTER, D. (1960), 'Conceptual structure in thought disordered schizophrenics', *Br. J. Psychiat.*, **106**, 1230.

— — (1962), 'The nature and measurement of schizophrenic thought disorder', *Ibid.*, **108**, 825.

— — (1965), 'The genesis of schizophrenic thought disorder. Re-test of the serial invalidation hypothesis', *Ibid.*, **111**, 377.

BERZE, J., and GRUHLE, H. W. (1929), *Psychologie der Schizophrenie* (Psychology of Schizophrenia). Berlin: Springer.

BINDER, H. (1936), *Zur Psychopathologie der Zwangsvorgänge* (A Contribution to the Psychopathology of Obsessions and Compulsions). Basle: Karger.

BRAIN, W. R. (1966), *Speech Disorders. Aphasia, Apraxia and Agnosia*, 2nd ed. London: Butterworths.

CAMERON, N. (1944), 'Experimental analysis of schizophrenic thinking', in *Language and Thought in Schizophrenia* (ed. KASANIN. J.). Berkeley: University of California Press.

CHAPMAN, L. J., CHAPMAN, J. P., and MILLER, G. A. (1964), 'A theory of verbal behaviour in schizophrenia', in *Progress in Experimental Personality Research*, vol. 1 (ed. MAHER, B. A.). New York: Academic Press.

CLARKE, P. R. F., WYKE, M., and ZANGWILL, O. L. (1958), 'Language disorder in a case of Korsakoff's syndrome', *J. Neurol. Neurosurg. Psychiat.*, **21**, 190.

CRITCHLEY, M. (1964), 'The neurology of psychotic speech', *Br. J. Psychiat.*, **110**, 353.

EAST, W. N. (1936), *Medical Aspects of Crime*. London: Churchill.

GOLDSTEIN, K. (1944), 'Methodological approach to the study of schizophrenic thought disorder', in *Language and Thought in Schizophrenia* (ed. KASANIN, J.). Berkeley: University of California Press.

HUBER, G. (1955), 'Das Wahnproblem, 1939–1954' (The problem of delusions, 1939–1954), *Fortschr. Neurol. Psychiat.*, **23**, 6.

— — (1964), 'Wahn, 1954—1963' (Delusions, 1954–1963), *Ibid.*, **32**, 429.

JAHRREISS, W. (1928), 'Störungen des Denkens' (Disorders of thinking), in *Handbuch der Geisteskrankheiten*, vol. 1 (ed. BUMKE, O.). Berlin: Springer.

KLEIST, K. (1914), 'Aphasie und Geisteskrankheit' (Aphasia and mental illness), *Münch. med. Wschr.*, **61**, 8.

— — and SCHWAB, H. (1950), 'Die verworrenen Schizophrenien auf Grund katamnestischer Untersuchungen. Teil II. Die denkverwirrten Schizophrenien' (The confused schizophrenias as seen in a follow-up study. Part II. The thought-confused schizophrenias), *Arch. Psychiat. NervKrankh.*, **184**, 28.

KRANZ, H. (1955), 'Das Thema des Wahns im Wandel der Zeit' (Secular changes in the content of delusions), *Fortschr. Neurol. Psychiat.*, **23**, 58.

LAWSON, J. S., McGHIE, A., and CHAPMAN, J. (1964), 'Perception of speech in schizophrenia', *Br. J. Psychiat.*, **110**, 375.

LENZ, H. (1957), 'Der Wandel des Bildes der Depression' (The change in the clinical picture of depression), *Wien. med. Wschr.*, **107**, 528.

MATUSSEK, P. (1953), 'Untersuchungen uber die Wahnwahrnehmung. 2. Mitteilung', *Schweizer. Arch Neurol. Psychiat.*, **71**, 189.

— — (1962), 'Untersuchungen über die Wahnwahrnehmung. 1. Mitteilung' (Investigations of delusional perception. Part I), *Arch. Psychiat. NervKrankh.*, **189**, 279.

MOWAT, R. (1966), *Morbid Jealousy and Murder*. London: Tavistock.

PAYNE, R. (1966), 'The measurement and significance of overinclusive thinking and retardation in schizophrenic patients', in *Psychopathology of Schizophrenia* (ed. HOCH, P. H., and ZUBIN, J.). New York: Grune & Stratton.

SCHMIDT, G. (1940), 'Der Wahn in deutchsprachigen Schriftum der letzten 25 Jahre' (The literature in German on delusions in the last 25 years), *Zentbl. ges. Neurol. Psychiat.*, **97**, 113.

SCHNEIDER, C. (1930), *Psychologie der Schizophrenen* (Psychology of Schizophrenics). Leipzig: Thieme.

— — (1942), *Die schizophrenen Symptomverbände* (The Schizophrenic Symptom Groups). Berlin: Springer.

SHEPHERD, M. (1961), 'Morbid jealousy: Some clinical and social aspects of a psychiatric symptom', *J. ment. Sci.*, **107**, 687.

SHURLEY, J. T. (1960), 'Profound experimental sensory isolation', *Am. J. Psychiat.*, **117**, 539.

WECHSLER, D. (1944), *The Measurement of Adult Intelligence*. Baltimore: Williams & Wilkins.

Chapter 5.   Disorders of Memory

ADAMS, A. (1959), 'Psychopathologie des Gedächtnisses' (Psychopathology of the memory), *Fortschr. Neurol. Psychiat.*, **27**, 243.

BLEULER, E. (1951), *Textbook of Psychiatry* (trans. BRILL, A. A.). New York: Dover Publications.

CONRAD, K. (1953), 'Zur Psychopathologie des amnestischen Symptomkomplexes. Gestaltanalyse einer Korsakowschen Psychose' (A contribution to the psychopathology of the amnestic symptom complex. Gestalt analysis of a Korsakoff psychosis), *Dt. Z. NervHeilk.*, **170**, 35.

— — (1953), 'Ueber einen Fall von Minuten Gedächtnis' (On a case of minute memory), *Arch. Psychiat. NervKrankh.*, **190**, 471.

GILLESPIE, R. D. (1937), 'Amnesia', *Archs Neurol. Psychiat.*, Chicago, **37**, 748.

O'CONNELL, B. (1963), 'Amnesia and homicide', *Br. J. Delinq.*, **10**, 262.

REISNER, H. (1957), 'Zur forensischen Problematik des Amnesieproblems' (A contribution to the forensic problems of amnesia), *Wien. Z. NervHeilk*, **14**, 28.

SCHNEIDER, K. (1928), 'Die Störungen des Gedachtnisses' (The disorders of memory), in *Handbuch der Geisteskrankrankheiten* (ed. BUMKE, O.), vol. 1. Berlin: Springer.

TALLAND, G. A. (1964), 'The psychopathology of the amnesic syndrome', in *Topical Problems in Psychiatry and Neurology* (ed. PETRILOWITSCH, N.), vol. 1. Basle: Karger.

— — (1965), *Deranged Memory. A Psychonomic Study of the Amnesic Syndrome*. New York: Academic.

WELFORD, A. T. (1951), *Skill and Age—An Experimental Approach*. London: Oxford University Press.

Chapter 6. Disorders of Emotion

ARNOLD, M. B. (1961), *Emotion and Personality*, vols. 1, 2. London: Cassell.

DEESE, J. (1964), *Principles of Psychology*. Boston: Allyn & Bacon.

FOULDS, G. A. (1965), *Personality and Personal Illness*. London: Tavistock.

HILLMAN, J. (1960), *Emotion. A Comprehensive Phenomenology of Theories and their Meanings for Therapy*. London: Routledge & Kegan Paul.

KRETSCHMER, E. (1928), 'Störungen des Gefuhlslebens. Temperamente' (Disorders of emotional life. Temperament), in *Handbuch der Geisteskrankheiten* (ed. BUMKE, O.), vol. 1. Berlin: Springer.

LEWIS, A. J. (1934), 'Melancholia: A survey of depressive states', *J. ment. Sci.*, **80**, 277.

— — (1936), 'Melancholia: Prognostic study and case material', *Ibid.*, **82**, 488.

MENDELSON, M. (1959), 'Depression: The use and meaning of the term', *Br. J. med. Psychol.*, **32**, 183.

ROTH, M. (1959), 'The phobic anxiety-depersonalisation syndrome', *Proc. R. Soc. Med.*, **52**, 587.

STÖRRING, G. E. (1964), 'Gefühlspsychologie und Psychiatrie' (The psychology of emotion and psychiatry), in *Topical Problems in Psychiatry and Neurology* (ed. PETRILOWITSCH, N.), vol. 1. Basle: Karger.

Chapter 7. Disorders of the Experience of the Self

ACKNER, B. (1954), 'Depersonalisation, I', *J. ment. Sci.*, **100**, 838.

— — (1954), 'Depersonalisation, II', *Ibid.*, **100**, 854.

FELDMAN, H. (1958), 'Zur phänomenologischen Strukturanalyse der Störungen des Ichbewusstsein' (A contribution to the phenomenological structure analysis of ego consciousness), *Arch. Psychiat. NervKrankh.*, **198**, 96.

KENNA, J. C., and SEDMAN, G. (1965), 'Depersonalisation in temporal lobe epilepsy and the organic psychoses', *Br. J. Psychiat.*, **111**, 293.

MEYER, J. E. (1959), *Die Entfremdungserlebnisse. Ueber Herkunft und Estehungsweise der Depersonalisation* (Alienation Experiences. On the Origin and Mode of Onset of Depersonalisation). Stuttgart: Thieme.

SEDMAN, G. (1970), 'Theories of depersonalization: A re-appraisal', *Br. J. Psychiat.*, **117**, 1.

— — and KENNA, J. C. (1963), 'Depersonalisation and mood change in schizophrenia', *Ibid.*, **109**, 669.

— — and REED, G. F (1963), 'Depersonalisation phenomena in obsessional personalities and in depression', *Ibid.*, **109**, 376.

WEITBRECHT, H. J. (1963), *Psychiatrie im Grundriss* (Outline of Psychiatry). Berlin: Springer.

WYRSCH, J. (1963), 'Psychopathologie, 1. Bedeutung und Aufgabe. Ich und Person. Bewusstsein, Antrieh und Gefühl' (Psychopathology, 1. Significance and task. Ego and person. Consciousness, drive and emotion), in *Psychiatrie der Gegenwart*, (ed. GRUHLE, H. W., JUNG, R., MAYER-GROSS, W., and MUELLER, M.), vols. 1, 2. Berlin: Springer.

YAP, P. M. (1965), 'Koro—A culture-bound depersonalisation syndrome', *Br. J. Psychiat.*, **111**, 43.

Chapter 8. Disorders of Consciousness

FELDBERG, W. (1959), 'A physiological approach to the problem of general anaesthesia and of loss of consciousness', *Br. med. J.*, **2**, 772.

JAHRREISS, W. (1928), 'Störungen des Bewusstseins' (Disorders of consciousness), in *Handbuch der Geisteskrankheiten* (ed. BUMKE, O.), vol. 1. Berlin: Springer.

STAUB, H., and THÖLEN, H. (1961), *Bewusstseinsstörungen* (Disorders of Consciousness). Stuttgart: Thieme.

Chapter 9. Motor Disorders

BOSTROEM, A. (1928), 'Störungen des Wollens' (Disorders of volition), in *Handbuch der, Geisteskrankheiten* (ed. BUMKE, O.), vol. 2. Berlin: Springer.

— — (1928), 'Katatone Störungen' (Cataronic disorders), in *Ibid.* (ed. BUMKE, O.), vol. 2. Berlin: Springer.

CHAPMAN, J., and McGHIE, A. (1964), 'Echopraxia in schizophrenia', *Br. J. Psychiat.*, **110**, 365.

FREEMAN, T., and GATHERCOLE, C. E. (1966), 'Perseveration—The clinical symptoms in chronic schizophrenia and organic dementia', *Ibid.*, **112**, 27.

KING, H. E. (1954), *Psychomotor Aspects of Mental Disease: An Experimental Study.* Cambridge, Mass.: Harvard University Press.

KRETSCHMER, E. (1961), *Hysteria, Reflex and Instinct* (trans. BASKIN, V., and BASKIN, W.). London: Peter Owen.

STENGEL, E. (1947), 'A clinical and psychological study of echo-reactions', *J. ment. Sci.* **93**, 598.

INDEX

INDEX

125

et, attention affected by, 82
– illusions resulting from, 17
– inability to change, 60
– paranoid, distractibility in, 82
– persecutory, 20–1
exual hallucinations, 25
– perversions, 108
hell-shock, 93
hort-term memory, 60
ign(s), primary, 8
illy cheerfulness, 73
leep, deprivation of, hypnagogic state in, 22
slowing down of time, 32
smell, hallucinations of, 25, 30, 44
smile, silly, in catatonia, 94
smiling depression, 75
snout spasm, 89
Sosias illusion, 64
spatial disorientation, 55
speech, confusion of, 54
— disorders of, 51–7, 94–100
— — functional, 52, 54–7
—— — in psychoses, 99–100
— flow of, 99
— mechanisms, 54–5
— movements, hallucinatory, 23
— pressure of, 36, 73, 99
— recognition, schema of, 54–5
Sperrung, 90
Stammering and stuttering, 52
Standard units, 33
States, manic, 72
— mixed affective, 72
Status epilepticus, 103
Stengel, on echo reactions, 95–6, 100
Stereotypies, 89, 91, 104
— definition of term, 94
— verbal, 37, 52, 56, 94, 100
Sthenic affects, 65
Stiff upper lip, 88
Stream of thought, disorders of, 35–7
Stupor, amnesia after, 103
— catatonic, 52, 91
— — mutism in, 52
— definition of term, 102
— depressive, 71, 104
— — mutism in, 52
— in fear, 86
— hallucinations in, 103–4
— hysterical, 102
— manic, 36
— occurrence, 102–3
— organic, 8–9, 104
— perplexed, 70

Stupor, psychogenic, 102–3
Subnormality, mental, 34, 95
— classification, 13
Subjective psychological experiences, 5
Substitution in formal thought disorder, 50
Suggestibility, 62, 63
Suggestion causing hallucinations, 20
Suicide, attempts at, 69, 85
— extended, 107–8
— risk of, 74
— threats of, 69
Sydenham's chorea, movements in, 93
Sylvian fissure, 30
Symbols, 49
Symptom(s), primary, 8
— hysterical, 6
Symptomatology, 1, 3
Syndromes, 7–14
— acute, 8
— amnestic, 7, 62, 72, 73, 82
— capgras, 63
— catatonic, 8
— chronic, 8
— subacute, 8
Systematization, 42

Tactile hallucinations, 29–30
Talking past the point, 52–3, 99
Taste, hallucinations of, 25, 30, 44
Telegram style, 56
Temporal disorientation, 32
— lobe disorders, 72 (*see also* Epilepsy)
— — — *déja vu* with, 63
— — — experience of time in, 32
— — — hallucinations in, 24, 30–1
— — — illusions in, 29
Tension, 67
Thinking, autistic, 34
— concrete, 49–50
— content of, disorders of, 39–48
— continuity of, disorders of, 36–7
— contrast, obsessional, 38
— desultory, 50–1
— difficulty in, in morbid depression, 71, 87
— disorders of, classification, 34–5
— form of, disorders of, 48
— healthy, features of, 50
— imaginative, 30
— inhibition or retardation of, 36
— pictorial, 63
— 'tramline', 7, 60, 62
— transitory, 50
— types of, 34
Thought, alienation of, 38–9, 80, 81